The Mama Memoirs

*Embracing Life, Relationships, and Identity While
Raising A Child with Special Needs*

By

Karen Richards

ISBN: 978-1-7328780-0-6 (paperback)

<u>DEDICATIONS</u>

To every Mama. Know you are fierce and amazing. Nobody can raise your kiddos quite like you can.

To every friend. Thank you for sharing a piece of this journey.

To all the unique children this book represents.

To my own parents. Thank you for showing me an amazing example of a loving marriage and being your child's protector.

To my husband Josh, my rock and partner in all that I do.

To Colton, Thalia, and Owen: my precious inspirations who make me who I am today.

FOREWORD

I officially met Karen Richards two years ago at a Chocolate Factory in St. Louis. We were both eager to goofily take photos, dressed in chocolatier gear, pretending to make the sweet treats… and decided to take them together! You know, two moms totally excited to be out for the night, acting like children! Many nights have since followed in similar fashion. From that night on, Karen and I both knew we were just the right kind of trouble when together. What Karen doesn't know (like, literally until she reads this), was that I unofficially started stalking her on social media one year prior to this first meeting.

Ok, that sounds totally creepy, but let me explain… One year prior to officially meeting Karen, I began a health transformation journey. As a busy pharmacist and mother of two young kiddos, I had put my health on the backburner for quite some time. But in January of 2015, I decided it was time to focus on myself and my health. Within the first month of starting my journey, I came across Karen's health coaching page and became obsessed with what she was sharing there. Not because it was overtly "clean and healthy" (I tend to fall in the healthy-ish category), but because she was REAL!!!

Karen was a real mama, sharing real-life tips. She was funny. She was genuine. She was helpful. And she was AUTHENTIC! And I don't know about you, but as a mom, I NEED real. Don't give me the overly-edited, perfect-lighting, never a stress in the world, nonsense kind of mama. I NEED the kind-hearted, working her tail off to do the best she can for her family, here to serve others, loving herself, choosing to go BIG in life, kind of mama to follow… and fall in love with. And so needless to say, one year later, I was overjoyed when I got to hang out with her in person and realized she was just as advertised: FUN, CARING, and FEARLESSLY AUTHENTIC! So, you can bet, when she shared that she was going to write a book to give us Mamas hope and guidance, I was ecstatic to see the amazing treat we would all soon have in store.

When my written copy arrived for review (after feeling so blessed to be asked to write this foreword for all of you) I was TERRIFIED. I'm not kidding! I stink at reading, like I fall asleep one-page in. It's like the words on the soft paper are a tranquilizer for me, and out I go. So, I do audiobooks. I am completely obsessed with having my buds in my ears with a book playing whenever I can. So, I thought, how in the world am I going to get through her sweet book in a reasonable amount of time to provide her and her readers with the meaningful and loving foreword this book so deserved (insert wide-eyed emoji face).

Well let me tell you… I did it! Like no joke, finished the entire book in two sittings. I couldn't put it down. I never fell asleep (even at night… with wine). I was totally entranced by the stories Karen was telling and the lessons she was sharing. Why? Not because it sounds like a fairytale. No! Because it is REAL! The book you are about to read is personal, it's a window into her world, it's the real deal. It is Karen's life as a mama. The ups. The downs. And all the lessons learned along the way.

Karen's accounts are entertaining, heart-warming, relatable, and honestly, at times scary, heart-wrenching, and raw. You will be in awe of the stories she shares and most definitely will walk away from each chapter with either a new perspective or a hands-on tip you can use in your life. You will laugh. You will cry. And you will probably wonder how on earth she has faced so many obstacles, and yet continues to want to give more, do more and be more not only for her family, but for the world around her. Quite frankly, I have no doubt that, just like me, you will fall further in love with Mrs. Karen Richards and her sweet family after reading these, The Mama Memoirs.

- Megan Martin, Founder and CEO of Conquer Career Counseling

Table of Contents

INTRODUCTION

Hi! I'm Karen. I'm a wife and a proud mother of three. I don't eat blue m&m's and I'm maybe a bit sarcastic… Kidding: I am *very* sarcastic. I am not a lawyer nor a licensed medical professional, so any advice I may give in this book is one hundred percent my own opinion. You might notice that I frequently refer to people *with* disabilities, but never disabled people. In our home, we know firsthand that people are so much more than their diagnosis.

I like to cuddle up with my softest blanket and a good cup of coffee or a crisp glass of Sauvignon Blanc when I read. Okay, okay, full disclosure: I like to sit with my softest blanket and a good cup of coffee or a crisp glass of Sauvignon Blanc even without a book. As an avid reader, I like to get lost in the words pretending I'm sitting with a girlfriend enjoying a wonderful conversation.

I grew up in small town Midwest America. Life was easy, overall. I played outside with neighborhood friends until it was dinner time in the school year or dark in the summer. I was involved in many extracurricular activities when I reached high school. My father was a research professor (a cloud physicist to be exact - you may want the Sauvignon Blanc if I try to explain *that* one to you), and we often traveled with him in the summer when he went to research facilities. These experiences with my family brought about an itch to travel way more frequently than just summer trips or Christmas vacations to see the grandparents.

Reading for me was an extraordinary escape. I imagined being on a raft with Tom Sawyer and Huckleberry Finn floating down a river. I wanted to explore where little Pip or David Copperfield grew up. Anne of Green Gables and Laura Ingalls Wilder sure seemed to have exciting things happening all the time! It drew me in and expanded my horizons without ever actually leaving home.

I invite you to do the same. Cuddle up, and let's have a little chat. I see you there, Mama… You might be feeling tired. Heck, tired probably doesn't begin to cover it. I see that you are overwhelmed. I can see the frustration and the worry lines between your eyes. As a matter of fact, your eyes look kind of sad. I see you.

Are you worrying about that upcoming medical appointment? The doctors keep telling you massive amounts of information to the point you can't seem to absorb it anymore, much less pass it on to concerned family and friends. You try to post on social media. Thank goodness for the comments from your friends that you can read when it gets late and you're feeling extra lonely. It's the only adult interaction you are probably getting, outside of chatting with hospital staff. Your friends used to play a much larger role in your social life. Maybe you are frustrated that the only mail you seem to get these days are medical bills. Have you and your spouse gone on a date anytime in the last few months? Better yet, have you gone on a date in the last year? Maybe your other children are demanding your attention, or you are feeling bad that you are not giving them enough time.

Can you relate to having postpartum depression? Maybe you can just relate to having depression in general. You most certainly do not have to be a parent to have experienced depression. Too many of our beautifully gifted young ones are struggling with mental illness these days, and it makes me so sad.

The stigmatism surrounding it makes one feel like they might be the only one feeling this way. Sometimes it may seem easier to just give up altogether. When I see a woman having struggles, I like to remind them that it's okay to not be okay. Feel those emotions. Learn from them. Just don't live in that space for extended periods of time. That is where longer term issues can arise.

The Mama Memoirs is not just about me and my story. It is not about my son and his story, or the story of our family. This story is about you. For some of you, this will reflect things that you have firsthand experience with, and perhaps it might bring a laugh because you can relate to my analogies of IEPs and dental visits. Perhaps you're currently walking through some of these hard times yourself. You are new to the world of whatever diagnosis has been handed to you and your family. Some of you, like me perhaps, searched the internet and self-diagnosed your child through WebMD with every rare form of anything and everything possible. You struggled to find anything in support of what you were trying to convey to your child's teacher or medical provider, trying to prove you knew what you were talking about. You knew something was off, but you could not quite put your finger on it - or maybe you knew exactly what it was but wanted to see if there were others out there like you, others who lived through what you are experiencing.

For many of you, you can relate to the emotions even if you don't have a child with a disability or chronic illness. Maybe you have walked through this with a friend or family member. Maybe you are a healthcare provider or a teacher, and my words might help you have more empathy for the story others are living each and every day. Perhaps it will open your eyes to their struggles or encourage you to engage in deeper conversations with them. Don't we all just want to be seen and heard? It might be hard to even imagine walking a mile in someone else's shoes when we can't understand what they have been through or what they are currently experiencing. That is where we get to practice empathy and compassion. Hopefully some of what I share in this book will help you to see the struggles of someone you care about or a family that you work with through a parent's eyes.

I really did not know what kind of book I wanted to write. Ever since my son Colton was born, people would tell me that I should write things down. The notes from the doctor's appointments, the funny things that he would say as a toddler. So, I did. Yet like many things in life, I just kept putting off writing my story. It was suggested that I write a short story and submit it to a magazine. I thought it was a great idea, I just did not know where to start. It was also suggested that I should start a blog, however the endless tasks of being organized enough to come up with creative content on a regular basis seemed overwhelming with all the other things that I had to do as a mom. *All the things*. Sometimes it is all the things that weigh us down, keep us feeling trapped and overwhelmed, and from just doing *one thing*. Sometimes one thing is all we need to do to move forward and feel better.

At the beginning of this summer, Colton started reminding me of a couple important milestones that were about to occur in his life. The first being that he would be celebrating his 18th birthday in August, right when he started his senior year of high school. That was a hard pill to swallow. How did I get to the point that I had an eighteen-year-old? A senior? We have been through many a hardship yet accomplished so much with him. However, as we began to attend senior class parent meetings, we were overwhelmed with what college might look like for him. It was going to be completely different than the typical student due to the physical, emotional, and mental challenges that he might have. I did not want to lose out on being able to share our journey up to this point.

I really wanted to journal this next phase of life, and as I began to do so I started rereading the many journals I had kept as Colton was a child. I had been meticulous in notating his stay in the NICU. For many years after, I had written down appointment dates and outcomes. I had journaled about when frustrations happened at school. When I started putting all the items together, the book just started to flow out quite naturally. All that was left for me to do was to fill in a few blanks on topics I thought might be helpful to others.

Another major event that happened this past summer, before I decided it was time to share my story, was a Leadership Retreat that I attended. An amazing woman, author, entrepreneur, and international speaker named Loren Lahav came to lead us through some practices to break through situations and excuses that might be holding us back from our life's desires. Loren lovingly, yet firmly, helped us guide ourselves into some self-reflection. Before we started to create a vision board, we wrote on the back of them a vision statement for ourselves. On mine, I proclaimed that I was an author that would be sharing a story. Not just any story, but *my* story about raising a child with a disability.

I had searched so often as a young mother for support or answers to questions that, most of the time, I could not find. I bought and enjoyed many books that shared the author's story of their child, however there was no practical advice for me to take from them. I did find some short books detailing some of my son's diagnosis, and from those I was able to decipher practical information. Very practical, very *dry* information. I decided it was time to write the book.

I wanted to intertwine my story with some comedic relief, as well as some tips for my readers. I also wanted it to be therapeutic for myself and to go back and say the things that I would have done differently if I could have. I know that I cannot go back in time and change anything, however I want to give my future self courage that I am the best advocate for my family and that I always need to remain brave enough to say what I believe to be true.

Writing was of the talents that I truly enjoyed as a child. Some of the friends that I grew up with may even remember sitting around my family's dining room table for Margaret Miller's Writer's Workshop. I have writings from many occurrences when I was a child. I wrote down my emotions when the space shuttle Challenger exploded. As a fourth grader, it helped me navigate through the feelings that I was having. I always kept a diary when I was in junior high and in high school. I journaled about experiences I was having, people that I would meet, places that I travel to. The heartache of young love, or the sadness of arguing with a friend. Venting out that my parents surely grounded me more than any other teenager on earth or that it was totally exciting that all the girls were getting together for a slumber party after the big football game that Friday night. Writing was a great expression for me.

Another talent that I feel I have is that of a coach. I have coached others in many aspects of life. I have taught fitness classes for years, as well as coaching cheerleading in the public-school system and owning my own private gym. It brought me great joy to watch my students grow and learn. When they would set a new tumbling goal or even tell me something they were working on in school, it made me so happy to see them reach that goal. It's brought me even greater joy to watch them grow into young adults, many of them married and now with children of their own. I can hardly explain the emotions that come about when a student I taught tells me they remember me saying something that has stuck with them or guided them in their lives. It is just priceless.

Today I enjoy a health coach practice where I get to help people find accountability in all areas of their life as well as become a better version of themselves. I help people to find exercises that they enjoy, and I get to coach them to discover ways to decompress and destress. I love getting to coach them on shopping excursions to learn to read food labels or a meal prep workshop. You can literally see light bulb moments, and it is fulfilling to see the things you have taught others help them and their families.

I know my most important talent. It is that of being a mother and wife, using the skills that God created me with to create an environment where everyone feels loved and nurtured. Where kind words are said often, and support is given always. I am not saying I agree with my hubby all the time or the kids don't make me want to pull my hair out, but my role is about love. It is also about being fearless and ferocious when it comes to doing what is best for my children and teaching them to speak up for others and to not only see injustices in the world but do something about it. That is why we created the Colton's Corner Foundation. There are those people that love to offer their opinions on the world, and there are those that put their heads down, get to work, and do something about it. A portion of every book sold will be going to the Colton's Corner Foundation so that *all* can feel included.

In several speeches I have given over the years, I ended with one of my favorite quotes by Erma Bombeck. I will leave this introduction with this:

"When I stand before God at the end of my life, I would hope that I would not have a single bit of talent left, and could say, 'I used everything you gave me'."

SETTING UP THE NURSERY

At some point after finding out you have a baby coming, the preparations begin. This is the exciting part of pregnancy. Today, I see so many cute things that I am *so* grateful did not exist during my three pregnancies. My poor husband. I can only imagine if I would have had Pinterest when I was pregnant with our first child. I can also imagine his thoughts. I can practically see him shaking his head while he grits his teeth with his eyes rolled all the way back up into his head. Yet he would want to amuse me. All the pins, all the boards, all the different colors and schemes and themes that could decorate my nursery. Pink or blue? Puppies or fairy princesses? Do you buy a cradle that turns into a toddler bed, and do we need a swing and a jumperoo thing? Do I carry him or her in a pack on my back or on my front? I probably will need multiple strollers because I exercise outdoors, go in small spaces indoors, and everything in between. I can picture all the beautiful things that I could put together to let our family know that we were expecting an addition to *our* family. All the fun of having a baby reveal party. Do you hit a baseball, or do you put colored cream in between layers of delicious cake?

What can I say? I have always been one that loves celebrations! Many a random day you will find me celebrating just being alive by sitting out on the deck with a group of girlfriends, drinking wine as we share tales of what is currently happening in our lives. I love birthdays! Especially my own and have been known to create my own birthday parties not for gifts, but just as a reason to gather people I love and care about around me. I love showering my friends with gifts and cards and little trinkets. Every February thirteenth I take a hint from one of my favorite televisions shows, Parks & Recreation, and I throw a Galentine's Day celebration. We have a pink drink that I spend a month selecting and taste testing, we have chocolates, sweets, and engage in fun conversation. I hand out swag bags at the end with fun little things like jewelry, makeup, essential oils, and candies.

In business, my team knows I tend to give random gifts, cards with Starbucks cards in them, or bling because they reached a new level. I was the one that wanted to throw all the bridal showers and baby showers for any and every friend that might need one. Halloween is my jam - I have been known to handout hot chocolate with spirits for the adults but that is not nearly as fun as St. Patrick's Day, as I come from a town that celebrates that very well! (Sidebar - it was a St. Patrick's Day Celebration that I took 35 sorority sisters home for that landed me my husband). I wish that Thanksgiving would go on for days and days and days. I love the fall season, seeing the leaves turn colors, pumpkin everything, watching the Macy's Day parade as the smells of pies and casseroles pipe out of the kitchen. Don't even get me started on Christmas. I am pretty sure even Alexa is rolling her eyes at me as I beg for holiday tunes to fill the air. I thread little sparkling twinkle lights in any space I can find, and the elaborate Christmas cookie baking begins. Scenes of snow falls on sugar cookies, colorful dishes to take to all the festivities, and researching to find the unique cocktail that will wow my guests! I'm willing to bet that if this book makes it to a certain friend back in my hometown, he will most certainly take a jab at me and my love for Christmas. There is nothing wrong with having Christmas lights up for an extended period of time, people!

As newlyweds, my husband had humored me by letting me send out little announcements when we first got puppies. That's right, friends. I said that I sent out birth announcements for my puppies. Those sweet black Labrador pups were the cutest things you can ever imagine. They were brother and sister and as dark as ebony. They had bright brown eyes and the sweetest spirits. I had to let everyone know, so I sent my news to everyone on our Christmas card list. It said something about the pitter-patter of little feet and then you opened the card and saw the picture of our new puppies. *Can you imagine?* The false hope I must have given family and friends! Can you imagine what this poor man was going to have to deal with when he found out that his wife was going to have an *actual* baby? I was overjoyed to say the least! I recall sharing the news with our families. I remember my younger brother walking into the local pizza parlor with balloons and a copy of the coveted book all pregnant women read as their pregnancy bible: What to Expect When You're Expecting. Of course, I read the entire book right away. I needed to know these things, I needed to know what was happening to my body every single moment of my pregnancy.

It is safe to say that no later than 6 weeks into my pregnancy, I had memorized every word of that book. I knew exactly what was going to happen for the next 34 weeks. When I first learned of my pregnancy my baby was only the size of a blueberry, but by week 15 my baby was the size of my fist. I was only going to be able to have one ultrasound during the pregnancy because that was all that was covered by my insurance at the time. It was scheduled for week 22, and it was then we would find out if we were having a boy or a girl. Oh, how that little nugget wiggled and hid! Tossing and turning, balling up as if he or she knew we wanted to know, yet they thought a surprise might be better. Luckily, the appointment after ours cancelled and our tech was kind enough to keep looking. Finally, the leg spread came, and the child that was now the size of a carrot was deemed to be a boy. We were told that everything looked perfect. Everything was going right as planned. He was actually measuring a little bit bigger than expected, but considering my husband had been a 10lb baby, they said that was totally normal.

To say that I was elated was an understatement. We had wanted a baby so badly. Some of my local friends had planned a baby shower for me, my husband's large extended family had planned a baby shower as well, and some of my mom's friends back in my hometown had planned a baby shower too! I was really looking forward to the silly games. Guessing what food was hidden in diapers, people wrapping a string around their middle to see if they can figure out the size of my pregnancy belly...Yet in that time of excitement, something was changing within me. I was not sure what was happening, but I knew that I started to feel different. I started having back aches. My book assured me that sometimes pregnant women will have such aches and pains, so I brushed it off. Then I begin to leak fluid. I decided I needed to get medical attention immediately.

I will never forget it as long as I live. It was a Sunday. I called for my OBGYN and was told that he was out of the country for a few weeks. Of course, he was; he did not have any patients that were due to have babies within the next two months. It was a great time to get out of town. They told me to head on over to the local hospital and go up to Labor & Delivery, and that they would run some tests.

This is the part where I would love to tell you they found what was wrong, kept me at the hospital, put me on bed rest, and gave me an antibiotic to fight an infection that I had. Unfortunately, that is not what happened. That is (as I was told several weeks after I delivered by my now returned-to-the-country OBGYN) what *should* have happened. So instead what happened was that I interrupted a golf game, a doctor came in and did a quick test, and told me that many first-time mothers do not know when something is wrong, and they panic. My chief complaint was that I was leaking what I believed to be amniotic fluid. I was assured that many times pregnant women drip urine out of themselves and do not even realize it's happening. It is perfectly normal, and it is okay that I came in. I should not worry, I should just go home and relax. It's hot outside, go for a swim. Everything will be fine.

So, I did. I went home, I relaxed, and continue to have lower back pain. I continued to leak this unknown fluid that I was told was urine. Now ladies, without being too graphic here, I believe for the most part most of us can tell the difference between when we need to relieve ourselves in the restroom and when Aunt Flo is coming for a visit. This was the latter. And now it was coming in major amounts. I called in to chat with the doctor's office one more time and was told if that was the only thing happening, be assured they had run tests at the hospital on Sunday and they all came back just fine. The tests showed that nothing was wrong. A week and a day passed. It was still very hot, so I went swimming at a girlfriend's home because my back was in excruciating pain at this point. The water did seem to relieve some of the tension in my back, so I was grateful for the pool time.

That year my husband was starting a new job as a teacher in the school district where we both grew up. At the time, we were living about 40 minutes away, and he was going to be commuting. I was working as the Director of a Chamber of Commerce. When I got to work on Tuesday morning, my back was so tight it was uncomfortable to sit down or stand up. I just could not find a comfortable position. I also was starting to have what I can only describe as menstrual cramps. I say this only because I did not know what labor pains felt like. After all, I was a first-time mother, so how could I know? The things that I knew were apparently wrong anyway. I consulted my book. My book, along with my secretary, agreed that at 27 weeks these could be something known as Braxton Hicks contractions. It would seem these fake labor pains were a way of your uterus preparing for the glory that is childbirth. Seemed rational enough. The best thing that I could do was try to slowly walk and that should slow them down or make them stop completely.

So, I did. Again. I followed my book's advice. I walked in circles around our large boardroom. The problem was that now my cramps were happening more often. I went to the bathroom and found that I was beginning to have spotting. After making the two other women in the office inspect the spotting with me, and agree this was probably not a good sign, I immediately called back to the doctor's office and was told they would page the doctor and call me back. At this point, my cramps were about 20 minutes apart. When I realized they were only about 10 minutes apart, I started to panic. No returned doctor calls. Who needs a doctor anyway? We all know who to call first in an emergency anyway right? No, I did not dial 911. I made a quick long-distance phone call to a real problem solver. I called my mother.

Remember how my hometown was about a 40-minute drive away? I don't know how she made it happen, but I'm pretty sure my mom was at my office within the next 5 minutes. Or so it seemed. We also made it that quick back to my hometown to the hospital, because the military base I worked near was closed to civilians at that time.

The next little part of the story here are only things that I have heard secondhand from my husband. Here he was at his new job as a middle school teacher, sitting on the very first day of orientation. He was excited because he also has football practice after orientation that day. This man breathes football, people. You have no idea.

Suddenly during part of his new teacher training, the principal appeared at the door and asked if he can speak to him in the hallway. Putting his hand on his shoulder, he explained to my husband that he needs to immediately get to the local hospital because his wife is in labor. Poor hubby. He was dumbfounded. He explained to the principal that the baby is not due until the week after Thanksgiving. It was only August 15th. The principal assured him that this was an emergency and he needed to leave immediately. Between him and my mother, they rallied the troops, and soon there were several family members there at the hospital. I don't know what their conversations were, however I do remember telling people that if they were crying or hysterical they would not be allowed in the room with me. I was very clear about that.

Call it luck, call it God's grace, call it whatever you want, I had been fortunate enough to have a sweet friend in college whose son had been born very premature. I knew the struggles she faced, but I also knew how amazing her son was. I also had a young girl that had been working for me have a baby come prematurely at the beginning of my own pregnancy, and I knew that he was healthy and strong. Even then I knew how important mindset was for things to go well, and I was not about to have chaos around me as my child entered the world.

Our church's deacon was in the hospital because his mother was having a procedure that day. We asked him to come up and see us. He laid his hands on my belly, and we all prayed over the safe delivery of our baby. I am glad I had those calming words of prayer over me, as well as *not* hearing the things that the doctors were telling poor hubs in the hallway. More details of his actual birth story will come in my chapter about spouse and marriage. I will say with the thoughts put into my husband's head, if you are a believer in the laws of attraction, be glad my attraction thoughts were stronger. I honestly did not come to find out for several more years the picture he was painted of doom and gloom. It has made me understand even more our different parenting styles, as well as why he was always asking me questions I thought strange and worrying more than I thought necessary about our son's expected life span.

So, like I had dreamed, there were baby showers. However, there was no pregnant mother at them. Instead, I was holding polaroids of my small baby, with tubes all over him, bruised like a prized fighter. His skin yellow from jaundice and so transparent and paper thin, you could see where sticky heart monitors and bandages were tearing layers away, leaving scars he still has today. There were no charming little fat rolls on his tiny, frail arms and legs.

I had dreamed of setting up a nursery, but instead I set up camp in the N.I.C.U. My dream of snuggling my newborn and smelling that new baby smell on his little head was exchanged for the nightmare of sitting bedside smelling only alcohol wipes and disinfectants. My dream of friends coming by to greet us after our return was replaced with the isolation of living pre-social media and feeling cut off from the world. A few visitors did come to the N.I.C.U. in those months, as well as my own mother and mother-in-law coming quite frequently. My exhausted husband, who now had started school and football season, drove the two hours up and back a couple times a week, as well as weekends. I was blessed by the fact that Colton's Godparents lived in St. Louis and had offered me somewhere to live so that I would not be at the Ronald McDonald house or sleeping in a hospital lounge. I was able to sleep a few hours a night in a comfortable bed and have a nice hot shower each day. Even so, my world seemed very dark. My beautiful celebration took a blow that has honestly taken years to process, heal, and recover from.

Things I Would Do Differently Today: The older and wiser Karen, who went on to have two closer to full-term pregnancies, would go back and tell the younger version of me to trust my instincts. I knew that there was something wrong. I verbalized it to medical professionals and believed they would understand what I was saying. When you have a gut feeling in your soul, Mamas, keep pushing. Go for another opinion. If you don't like that answer, get another opinion. Make them redo the test. If you still don't like it, do it again or go somewhere else. I should have pushed more. I would not trade my amazing child with special needs for the world, however I do wish I would have been more aggressive in asking them to redo tests instead of blindly believing what I was told because I was a "first-time mother and many first-time mothers just don't know what they don't know." I did know. My body knew. My heart knew. But my brain chose to believe someone else. Believe your heart.

AFTER BIRTH

It is my perception that the greater percentage of couples have an amazing after birth experience. The doctor has a parent or birthing partner cut the umbilical cord. You hear of people popping the champagne as family and friends gather near, bringing in flower arrangements, colorful balloons, and showering this new life with presents galore. Siblings or other young family members come in to greet the new life. Pictures are taken, home videos recording the joyous moments, or nowadays pictures immediately posted to social media for all the world to see. It is a monumental occasion that is worthy of such celebration.

My birth experience most certainly was not like that. There were so many people in the room, I lost count. Teams switched in and out. They kept working on me, trying to slow the progression and get me stable enough to be flown out to St. Louis, where it would be safer if I delivered this early. I had just made it to my 27th week. An entire trimester too early. When it became apparent that they were not going to be able to stop labor, the helicopter that had been called for me was sent back.

There was now a team of doctors there for me, as well as a team of doctors for my baby. I asked for my family doctor, because she did have nursery privileges and I had planned on her continuing his care. They almost laughed at my request. However, I did take their advice (at the urging of my husband who had been coached in the hallway prior) that we would want a pediatrician, because they specialize in infants. They had made it very clear to my husband that this would be a process where they would be trying to revive our baby, and we would want him to be with someone who at the very least had intubated a baby recently. Looking back, this probably was one of the better suggestions we took, since so far most of the medical advice was not turning out so hot.

I was told that after he was born and stabilized, they would then call a new helicopter that would transport him. At the time, I never put two and two together that they were waiting until he was stabilized because they never believed he would survive.

I had not had an epidural, and as the pushing process began I was given Demerol through my I.V. It really knocked me out, but I do remember my husband asking how I was going to push if I seemed to be unconscious. The doctor assured him I would, and it would help keep me calm. I was calm all right. I was high as a kite! I now personally feel I was drugged so that when Colton was born not breathing, I might be too looney to get hysterical.

After he was born and whisked away for trauma care, and my placenta was delivered and whisked away on it's own trip down to the pathology lab, I found myself all alone. Josh was exactly where I wanted him to be: following our baby. Everyone else followed him. Anxious friends and family members sat on pins and needles outside the nursery, waiting to hear updates. I laid in a bloody bed, forgotten. I had no idea what was happening with my newborn, nor did I really understand what was happening to me. As I laid there alone with my thoughts, I remember thinking *I wonder if I will ever meet him? I wonder if someone will bring me in a wheelchair down to the nursery with everyone else so that I can see what is going on? I wonder what is happening **right now**?*

After what seemed like hours, an angel appeared to me. Now this was not a winged angel with a glowing light shining from her hovering halo, nor a direct line to the heavens above. This angel appeared to me in the form of a hospital volunteer. Yup. A candy striper. She never told me her name, but she had to be nearing the age of my elderly grandparents. Her light gray hair was meticulously done in curls that reminded me of my beautician grandmother who, up until her death, enjoyed her hair done weekly. She was small in stature and had a slight hump in her back. Her walk was more of a shuffle than a stride. I'm not sure if she came in the room to offer me water or to bring a magazine, but whatever the cause, she could tell that I was in dire need.

She came over and placed her soft wrinkly hand on mine and asked if I needed anything. I do not even remember answering her, but I do remember what followed next. She helped me up and together we shuffled to the bathroom where she instructed me to clean myself up, and when I came back in the room she had pulled the disgusting sheets off the bed and said that a nurse was coming to help move me to a different room. After I was moved to another room, I at least felt cleaner and had fresh sheets. The angel appeared to me again, bringing a cheeseburger and French fries. Thank you, sweet baby Jesus. *"I'm sure you haven't eaten in quite some time, and I don't know if this is something you would eat but I took a guess."* That was the best tasting thing I had consumed in I don't know how long.

Considering that my son made his appearance at 1:30 in the afternoon, it was now well past the dinner hour, and no one had been back to see me or tell me what was going on, you can imagine the things that were swirling in my head. Finally, Josh returned. He had a couple of polaroids to share that were frankly terrifying to look at. It really did not look like a baby. Some small little mass of flesh with tubes all over. It had taken a long time, but they had gotten our son stabilized, and the plan was to fly him to St. Louis to a Level 1 Trauma Center. A sense of relief washed over me.

Things started to happen very quickly. People came into the room pushing forms for us to sign, different doctors and nurses telling us the part they had played and what likely steps would occur when their counterpart at St. Louis Children's Hospital admitted him in. Finally, the air ambulance helicopter team showed up.

As they were preparing him to leave, one of the nurses came in to talk to me. Possibly by my wild, deer in the headlights eyes, she had the good sense to ask me if I had even seen the baby. In all the commotion, she was the first one that had bothered to ask. My eyes welled up and I shook my head no. She said, *"Looks like take off time is going to be adjusted then."*

Minutes later an incubator was wheeled into my room. My little man, my Colton, was wrapped up like a mummy in gauze, ready to take his first flight. All that I could see was a bright pair of steel blue eyes looking back at me. And just like that, he was gone.

My husband and mother-in-law drove up that night to meet him there at the hospital. My mother left to go run errands and try to prepare for being gone for a couple days, as my father was out of the country on business. Once again, I was left to lie alone with my thoughts. What a scary place to be.

The next morning, I awoke very early. A close friend's mother was sitting on my bed. She brought me a single rose and words of encouragement. She had a daughter with disabilities that was a few years younger than my friend and me. She shared how much further modern medicine had come and ensured me my baby was in good hands.

I've probably never thanked her for that visit. But what I have done is paid it forward. I've shown up hospital bedside for preemie births, for friends that had dying parents, and for children that have spent too much time in the hospital, as well as some that never got to go home.

It's hard. It brings up hard memories. I mean seriously, who wants to hang out in a hospital? But do you know what would be harder? Knowing I could have offered them some shred of encouragement or just made the situation easier because they had someone to talk to, but instead doing nothing. Even if I could not stay, what if I had dropped by a book, some fresh fruit, or a coffee? For those of you who haven't experienced this, please take the time to read through the tips in the Say Something or Say Nothing chapter. For those of you that are in these moments now, even though there is little for someone to do, sometimes this is all they have to offer. They want to help but they don't know how. Be forgiving of them for not knowing. It is also good to give yourself a little reality break, if at all possible.

Now back to that morning. Soon after my friend's mom left, my own mother arrived, ready to drive me to be with my son. I let a nurse know that if the OBGYN that had delivered my baby didn't show up soon, I would be walking out of the hospital against medical advice. She must have relayed my message or he must have been on his way in, because he quickly came. Without many words, he wrote me a prescription for painkillers and was gone. Just like that. After discharging my mom took me to Kmart pharmacy to pick up the meds, where we saw said doctor again, with his children. He didn't say a word to me. Maybe he was smarter than I gave him credit for.

Things I Would Do Differently Today: Well, for one, I would have pushed my nurse's button and demanded that cheeseburger sooner! Ha! All humor aside, I wish I would have had an action plan in place. I now have a living will as well as a medical directive. With future pregnancies, I did make a birthing plan with action steps for if things went smoothly or an action plan for if things went awry. I never thought about having a birthing plan for my first child. I was so caught up in following along in my 'pregnancy bible' that it never occurred to me that things may not go as planned. I urge all parents to have a living will and medical directives in place for you and your spouse at the very least. As hard as it sounds, it would not hurt to have medical directives in place for your children as well. If you travel often for business, if your kids travel for sports, heck, if you leave a hospital for a couple hours, a medical directive can really help the doctors, nurses, and support staff caring for your loved one to know what to do. It also allows you to take some time to clearly plan things out when you are calm, rational, and not trapped in the emotion of a traumatic experience.

NAVIGATING THE NICU

After the car ride to St. Louis, I was anxious to see my son. I found my husband in a waiting area. He told me that a baby near ours was having a procedure done, so everyone was cleared out. It might be a couple hours yet. Are you kidding me? It hadn't even been 24 hours since my active labor began, but it felt like an eternity. I needed to see my baby.

Remember, other than seeing Colton's eyes and wrapped up body, I had only seen the few polaroids as this was pre-cell phone camera era. Josh did not even have a cell phone yet, so there was nothing he could have sent me via text or email. He showed me the couple of new Polaroid photos the nurses had taken upon Colton's arrival. His mom had taken pictures on her regular camera, but of course in those days she would need to finish out her roll and take it to a photo lab to be developed.

After many tears from me and what seemed like hours, a nurse came out to prep me for meeting my son. Ahhh...the next Angel. Her name was Judy, the same as my mother. Nurse Judy very quickly became the single most important person in my life. A 27-year veteran in the nursing profession, she could make residents rethink their actions with only a raised eyebrow. She made cassette players to put in Colton's incubator appear and found all kinds of cute decorations to place all over the outside of it. It was even decorated from Colton to me on my birthday, complete with a real cake (minus candles due to the oxygen). I could call her after I left about midnight each night, when I needed to know at 3am how his feedings had gone or at 6am when I woke for a progress report prior to coming over to the hospital. She made sure if she was not on those shifts, she personally introduced me to the nurse coming on duty so I would trust my little preemie was in good hands. I often think of her and wish we had stayed in touch longer.

When the time came to meet Colton for the first time, Nurse Judy was the one who prepared me with humor. I think she had a sense that humor was going to be key in his upbringing. *"I know your little fighter might look rough Mama, but I promise the other guy looks worse. He will be okay though, I have a feeling about this one."*

Even though she had given me the pep talk, I wasn't prepared. No longer wrapped in gauze, he was laid out in an open bed with nothing on but his birthday suit. He was too tiny for a diaper, only a little tent covered his boy parts. His skin was so translucent I could see his veins. What he did have was his Daddy's exact shaped head, with loads of dark hair like his mama. It was hard to look as Nurse Judy gently described to me what all the different tubes in his nose, arm, belly, and even head were for. She pointed out heart monitors, blood pressure cuffs, and told me why his little eyes were covered (to block the blue light looming above him to help with his jaundice). It was overwhelming.

He had a respirator breathing for him, but within 24 hours he was downgraded to a CPAP machine. They were hopeful that after a few days he might be doing so well that he could be downgraded again just to oxygen through a nose cannula. But, he failed that test miserably. I had another sob fest right there in the N.I.C.U.

It was then that another sweet nurse came to my aide - those nurses! Always so intuitive! She asked if I had ever held Colton yet. I had been too scared to ask. She said it really would be no problem and I watched her quickly unplug everything, whip him right out of his incubator, and reattach everything in one fell swoop as she held him practically in one hand.

She wrapped him up tight and handed him to me! Oh my, he was so tiny. I felt like I was holding an empty blanket. We took pictures so people could see in comparison. Josh stretched a $5 bill over him. He was not a whole lot bigger. His dad's wedding ring could go all the way up his thigh without touching.

These may not be the type of pictures that you want to blast all over social media, however it is really important to take pictures of your baby. One day you will be so happy that you did. We have one typical nursery picture of our daughter, and by the time our second son was born they did an amazing photo shoot right there in the hospital. But our N.I.C.U. pictures are just as precious. For us, it is a great reminder of everything that he has overcome. For some parents, those pictures might be the only memory that they have.

Sometimes his alarms would go off, signifying that his tiny little heart had dropped low or stopped all together. Panic would set in as I watched nurses calmly wait a moment to see if he could get his act together on his own. Sometimes they would walk over and just give him a good flick on the foot and say "*Stop that*" and boom! His heart would start right back up.

Soon enough, I was able to be like those nurses. I was learning his patterns. For instance, if he was given a feeding tube meal, he usually would decide that he did not want to breathe. A full belly meant that it was time to just relax a little too much. I think of us as adults, flung out over furniture after a large holiday meal. The only difference is our brain is developed enough to know to breathe. He was being given high doses of caffeine straight into his little IV to make sure his brain stayed perked up like he had drank six or seven cups of piping hot Starbucks.

I cannot say enough about the nurses we met while we were there. Befriend them. They are your best resource of information. Charts get passed from residents, to attending physicians, and sometimes on to fellows. They discuss cases and check in during rounds. Nurses are in the trenches, though. I think of the doctor as a captain of a ship yelling out orders to his crew, however without the crew the ship would never move. There would be no one to man the sail, swab the deck, and man the galley. Everyone would starve, or the ship would sink.

I wanted to make sure I kept a close watch on this crew, because they seemingly always had all the good info. It served me well to befriend as many of the nurses as I could. These men and women will be your lifeline in the N.I.C.U. or any other hospital event. They taught me many things on how to care for my new little baby, they were always happy to answer my questions, and they made me feel more at ease with whatever news the doctor was delivering that day. They helped me to become an expert on my own baby.

Even though I did not get to take him home the day he was born, now I almost cannot imagine if I had! With my other two, I had already learned so much from my first. It is no wonder so many new mothers get the baby blues. It is completely overwhelming to figure out your first baby and start to anticipate their needs. This is why I feel it is so important that you become an expert about your loved ones. You know better than anyone else the sounds that they make when they are happy or uncomfortable, you are the only person that will know what their true baseline is because there will be shifts of people coming through that only see your child at certain times. As you learn the mannerisms of your child, it helps you to advocate even better for them.

I also learned to ask for things. You are paying a *ridiculous* amount of money if you have a loved one in the hospital. I can not stress that enough. *Ridiculous.* Some items are very well documented. Some are not as well documented. If you have befriended your nurses and staff, probably even less items are documented.

I saw once on an insurance benefits statement that I had been charged $55 after the birth of my daughter for Tylenol. *Wait. What?!?!* Do you know how many bottles of Tylenol I could go out and buy for $55? It is preposterous. No thanks on the Tylenol, I will save that money for diapers for a couple weeks. Again, here is part of what is wrong with our healthcare system today!

But the nurses would bring extra baby soaps when he eventually got to the point we could bathe him, gave me hospital blankets to take home because they are the best for swaddling, and other little things like this little cushion volunteers had made so he did not slide down the propped up mattress.

They also made sure I was well fed. The hospital Colton was in had a program where if you breastfed your baby, you could get three free meals a day on a hospital tray brought up to you. It made complete sense, they wanted to make sure they were meeting my dietary needs because that way they knew that my baby was getting higher nutritional value in his breast milk. I cannot imagine if on top of everything else, I would have had to purchase three meals a day sitting in the N.I.C.U. for that long. It was much better food than the couple of fast food places down in the cafeteria.

If you have a child that has a hospital stay, be sure to look into parent trays. Sometimes they are free, and sometimes there is a cost associated with them, however the nutritional value of what you get from many hospitals is way better than if you continue to run out to fast food or bring in prepackaged foods to snack on. You will need your strength and energy! Also, many times you can get a lot of food for a little bit of money. Say a tray only cost $5 or $6 and you are able to get a salad, an appetizer, multiple sides of fruits and vegetables, a meat, a dessert, and more than one drink. You might end up being able to get a couple apples or something you can snack on in between meals.

Another tip is to designate one person to share your news. It was so helpful to me back in the days without social media that I was not bombarded with requests to see how Colton was doing. Anytime someone called the N.I.C.U. I would be called out to the front desk to receive the message, and then I would have to decide if I wanted to call that person back long distance. To avoid spending that much time away from Colton, I called in to my secretary every single morning so we could go over what was happening at work, and I would give her an update on his progress. That way all the people back home were asking her if they were curious, and she was happy to share the news for me.

Things I Would Do Differently Today: This is a hard one, because most of the time when a hospital visit occurs, you have no idea that it is about to happen. You don't know whether you will be there for a day, a week, or for months to come. Once the first visit happened though, I was better prepared for the many future stays in the hospital, both for my child and for myself. I would say being able to take a few things from home if your child has a private room might help to make them feel calmer. A fun pillowcase, a stuffed animal, or a framed picture. Any of these items might help your loved ones. For me, it is always important as a parent to take a few self care items along. A book, some essential oils, a pack of cards. Something to help pass the time as days turn into weeks sometimes. As I mentioned, befriending the nurses was super helpful so that is something I would still continue to do, but I would continue a relationship longer with the few I really connected with because they become great advocates for you.

POSTPARTUM DEPRESSION

Well friends, here comes the hard part. This is a part of me that I really don't want to dive into. I have been more open sharing this in recent years because I find it so important to empower other women. Writing this book has been therapeutic for me in my journey. There have been times I had to pause because I wasn't sure if my writer's block was due to me forgetting the events or my unconscious trying to suppress them.

Our minds never really forget traumatic experiences, no matter if they are physical or emotional. Sometimes they manifest and present as physiological symptoms. Sometimes they manifest as an entirely different set of emotional suffering.

I want women to feel safe talking about postpartum depression or depression in general. Being a Mama is hard no matter the circumstances. We all have our own crosses to bear, and no matter what you think of another woman while looking in from the outside, you do not know what she is feeling. We can not shame her for creating whatever reality her experiences have brought her to.

I was never one that joined a lot of support groups, mostly because I suffer the personality of an extreme empath. I take on the hopes and dreams of others, but I also take on their heartache and their suffering. Sometimes it was hard for me as a mother to connect with other mothers that might be in similar situations, because I feared the heartache I was silently suffering would be multiplied and compounded so large that I could not deal with it. I had already suffered through postpartum depression after bringing my child home from the hospital and having to stay indoors all winter.

Although there were many other parents in the N.I.C.U. that were having the same experiences, I found it hard to want to connect with them. We made small talk in the lounge at the hospital when I stepped out for a bathroom break or something to eat, but I did not create any meaningful relationships with other N.I.C.U. parents.

Even after returning home, I am sure that I offended many a family member or friend because the doctors had explained how important it was that we not expose the premature lungs of our baby to germs, as he was coming home during the onset of cold and flu season. Catching something like RSV could be deadly to him. When we sent out Colton's baptismal invitations we even placed a statement on it: Please kindly leave your kids and colds at home. I was told that statement offended a few. I couldn't be concerned with that. I wasn't concerned with anything but the health of my baby. We were holding a private Mass and baptismal ceremony so that he would not be exposed to a church full of well meaning well-wishers carrying germs. We also were only inviting a small group back to our home after the ceremony where I immediately handed everyone Germ-X upon entering.

I was overwhelmed with anxiety as I thought of places I needed to go and errands I needed to run. Danger lurked everywhere. I did not want to go to church or to Walmart because I might bring germs home and infect my child. I became paranoid, wanting my husband to change clothes as soon as he came home from school each day because I just knew all those middle schoolers and football players were covered in some sort of rare infectious disease he would surely pass on to our immune compromised baby. The imaginary terrors began to drive me even deeper into a dark place.

I am a person that thrives in my health when I get enough vitamin D (hence why I now travel to a beach every few months. I enjoy it for so many reasons but health-wise, I need it), and without it I most definitely suffer seasonal depression. S.A.D.,seasonal affective disorder,is a true depression disorder that many people suffer from during late fall and winter. Combine it with the postpartum feelings I was having, and it is little wonder that I was a mess! I was sad, angry, and frustrated. My sleep schedule was completely out of whack, and the exhaustion from driving back and forth to work and medical appointments when Colton first came home didn't help.

My home was not even the comforting safe haven that I had envisioned. Instead, it was an extension of the N.I.C.U., smelling like alcohol wipes and disinfectant. With all the therapists that came through, I was constantly cleaning and wiping down everything. I might as well have placed him in a bubble.

Even when I would take him to the local pediatrician for check-ups, we sat out in the hallway by their exit door so that when it was our turn we could be brought in from the back and he would not be exposed to any children or parents in the waiting room. Even that was tough. I appreciate that today I am seeing more and more pediatricians offices have two separate waiting areas for "sick child" visits and those there for "well child" visits.

For me, not being able to make eye contact with another mother who might give me a knowing smile as my baby cried seemed like just one more thing I was missing out on. Or to see little toddlers running around reading books and playing with toys, so that I could imagine my son getting to that stage. It was a very lonely time. The only time I felt like I went outside was to get mail, and since my mailbox was attached to the house right by the front door, I did not get very far. That winter seemed to be a long one. We had moved home, but most of my friends had moved away after high school. It was hard to feel so isolated. Our parents, while appreciated, were about the only social circle we had.

Maybe this is you. Perhaps you're unable to leave the home because it is easier sometimes just to stay in and take care of your child. Or maybe you are not like me at all. Maybe you have been able to venture out and join groups where you find love and support. This is my hope for all of you. Over the years I have met some amazing parents whose children are unique, spirits full of joy, and they themselves are inspirational to others around them. I am so glad that I have been able to listen to their experiences and share my own. Some of these parents have been through the tragic heartache of losing their child after months or years of medical care.

It matters. It matters as parents to have a connection. It matters to have a community of people that can understand and empathize with you. It matters to have people who hear your story and you give them hope or for you to get hope from theirs. We should never feel embarrassed or ashamed that we need someone to help us. A couple of websites that you can go to in order to learn more about mental health are: http://www.mentalhealth.gov and http://www.nimh.nih.gov . Especially if you are feeling hopeless, lost, or overwhelmed, I encourage you to just check these sites out and see if you might relate to the information they are sharing.

Things I Would Do Differently Today: I would not have felt so bad about the fact that I needed help. I definitely would have gone to a medical provider sooner about depression. I knew something was wrong, but I had a lot of shame around the way that I was feeling. I remember the relief I felt when I finally told my family doctor about the overwhelmed feelings I was having. As a mother herself, she was quick to reassure me that I was not alone. Those words brought me a lot of comfort.

I had been connected to a couple other moms with young ones, and they both were taking medication for their postpartum depression. Here is the thing - I do not think ANYTHING negative about those other mothers. I don't know why we, as women, are so terribly brutal on ourselves. We are our own worst enemy many times.

I also think I would have sought out a therapist. My family doctor was fabulous not only to share with me that I was not alone, but she truly talked me off the proverbial ledge I had mentally placed myself on. I had one of my crying breakdowns in her office. I had tried so hard to hold it together for the last seven months. I felt weak and tired, but I guilted myself into thinking I should be strong and have my act together. I would most definitely not shame myself today for feeling so sad and alone. You shouldn't either.

MEDICAL DEBT

Holy Crap, Batman. The hubs and I were plugging right along in life. He was, as earlier mentioned, a public school teacher. Although that wage might support a young couple with no children, teachers with families are left feeling severely underpaid. Can I get an Amen?

I had been working a full-time job as well, but it did not pay the best salary. I would estimate that between the two of us, we were grossing only around $40,000 a year. Living in a fairly low cost area, making one car payment, we were still living fairly comfortably. We were already expecting an increase in living costs once the baby came, because hello! Have you seen those cute Adidas superstars in a size one? We would need one of those jumpy things and tons of diapers. We were prepared for all the typical expenses, or so we thought. But we never expected to start Colton's life off with a hospital bill that would make you literally vomit.

One of my high school cheerleaders helped her Dad (who held the insurance policies for the school system Josh worked in) organize the medical files of the staff and their families. She once shared with me at cheerleading practice one day that, while most families had only a folder or two, we had an entire file cabinet for Colton. He had not even celebrated his first birthday yet. Talk about an eye opening conversation. I was starting to truly understand the depth of what our medical debt was becoming.

After the initial sticker shock wore off, I decided that I needed to know every single part of his medical bills. I asked for an itemized statement of his 60-day NICU stay. This was quite an eye-opening experience. I discovered the floor space and incubator alone had incurred a rental fee near $1,700 per day. Thus far in our twenty year marriage, we have never paid a rental fee nor mortgage amount that high for a single *month*. I guess this would be a great place to insert more about what is wrong with healthcare in America, but that honestly could be a book in itself.

This was back in the year 2000. I'm not sure what the going rate is for floor space now, however from what I have seen, the N.I.C.U.s of today have been upgraded considerably compared to what we experienced. As a matter of fact, significant changes were being made to the N.I.C.U. at St. Louis Children's Hospital during our time there. When our son entered as a new patient, it was loud and noisy. Alarms beeped, and various medical equipment dinged. The lights were bright, and everything was white and sterile. Yet by the time we graduated, parts were being painted darker, and the noisy chimes and dings were being replaced by soft lights. There were beautiful rooms for mothers to pump in rather than walking down an outside hall feeling like we were headed to the dairy barn. It was a much more inviting environment. Things seemed softer. It caused everyone to speak quieter. I felt more relaxed, which not only affected my own health, but that of my little fighter.

But I digress, back to the medical debt. After 60 days in the N.I.C.U., we were released to go home. We decided to stay with my parents for a short time. I was mentally and physically drained. I needed emotional support, not to mention physical support. Within a couple days, it was like my body's fight or flight response let go of all the fight. I was so sick. I slept for several days, only being woken up from time to time to eat and pump breast milk.

Even though we had been released from the hospital, our time there was far from done. Our baby was in for a slew of medical visits. Several times a week I drove the two hour drive back to the hospital. He was seeing an eye specialist almost weekly, due to retinopathy of prematurity (for those of you who do not know, this is why Stevie Wonder is blind. He was born premature and had the same eye condition as Colton). We were also seeing a cardiologist weekly because he had been diagnosed with pulmonary stenosis as well as a significantly sized heart murmur. We were being seen in the "Preemie Clinic" every other week, just to make sure that he was growing on time due to feeding issues.

Our N.I.C.U. bill had not even arrived yet. However, we had already been told that we made too much money to receive any kind of State Assistance. Remember that whopping teaching salary?

Immediately after we got home from the N.I.C.U., we were set up with early intervention. The First Steps program was amazing for us, and I will forever be grateful for the therapists that came in our home. It is a program based on early intervention services from birth to age three for children with disabilities, cognitive challenges, or like him - automatically accepted due to having a grade two brain hemorrhage at birth that could cause learning delays. His therapy list included a physical therapist or her PTA that came in twice a week, an occupational therapist twice a week, a speech therapist twice a week to help with oral therapy and feeding issues, and a behavioral specialist that came once a week in the beginning, and eventually slowed to monthly visits right before he turned three. All these therapies began for a two month old baby who was also being driven back to the hospital two to three times a week.

Somewhere around Christmas, my Board of Directors at the Chamber of Commerce decided that I needed to move back into the county where my job was (we had been living in our hometown since Colton's homecoming). With all the medical treatments that the baby was getting, I just did not feel I could move away from my support system yet. At that time they decided that I was not fulfilling my job requirements, and they let me go.

I will never forget walking into my home the day before Christmas Eve and telling my family that I had just lost my job. Devastated does not even begin to describe it. I never had any intention of being a stay-at-home mother. In fact, my husband and I had discussed that perhaps as our family expanded, I might be the primary breadwinner and he might be an at home dad, as long as he could continue to coach.

Up to this point, I had somehow managed to be there for every single one of Colton's specialist, therapist, and doctor appointments, while driving back and forth 40 minutes to my job. I had just lost the one thing that I felt I actually had control over.

I also lost my contribution to our household income, and the piles upon piles of bills were starting to trickle in. It was not only Christmas, but almost the top of the year where we had to meet deductibles before insurance kicked in. I was on Cobra healthcare from my husband's previous job, still waiting for new enrollment in January.

I'm going to start telling you some of the good, along with some of the bad, advice we got right here (instead of waiting until the "What I Would Do Differently") because, financially speaking, *I promise you* nothing haunts me worse today or continues to cause stress on both my husband and I than this piece of the equation. No, money cannot buy you happiness, but it sure can pay the medical debt.

Our pediatrician actually was more helpful than most people I would consider "financial experts." He told me to just pay a small amount monthly, even as the bills increase. Yes, creditors would call, but just always pay something. I did not need to live in fear that he would cut my child off as a patient (which was my concern). He said hospitals, etc. will end up charging off some of the debt sometimes after they have collected what they can. I wish I would have gotten his advice sooner, as we had already been racking up medical debt on our credit cards. Yikes. What a mistake. Hospitals typically don't add interest for bills. Send them $5 if that's truly all you can, but have a paper trail that each month you are trying.

Do not put any medical debt, medical equipment, hospital payments, etc. on credit cards. The interest alone was killing us, yet we foolishly believed if we did not purchase certain items or pay medical bills, we would be ruined. Well, we really ruined ourselves and set ourselves up for many years of financial disaster. I don't say this to frighten anyone, just to bring awareness that there are better routes. Sometimes when we are in overwhelmed mode, we don't think of these things. So again I implore you, do not put any medical debt onto a credit card!

By the time Colton was about 18 months old, my husband applied for a head coaching position at a neighboring school district. Within a week, we got the great news: He got the job! We truly believe God was watching over us, because within a week of his new hire we got a letter from our current insurance group that Colton had exceeded the lifetime maximum of 2.5 million dollars, and they were booting him off our plan.

I know there are a lot of things wrong with our current healthcare system today. I am not going to tell you that I'm a believer that Obamacare is the best thing since sliced bread. I also don't believe it to be the worst. What it means for families like ours, who are not on a group plan, is that they can no longer be denied coverage due to a pre-existing condition. I also am not talking about the generally healthy people who are paying outrageous premiums. I get that. It sucks. I am talking about the parent of a baby less than two years old with multiple major health challenges who has been removed from the insurance plan. Had that been a lifetime sentence for us, I'm not sure how we could have continued on. You see how people are literally forced into poverty and to rely on SSI or disability insurance because working and having a decent income actually penalizes them more.

After paying out of pocket for several months before changing insurance plans, and then accruing more medical debt over the next three years, we found ourselves starting to panic. We were renting a 2 bedroom/1 bath almost 900 square foot cottage after having lived in a large beautiful home prior to his birth. We actually had been in the buying process when he was born, but backed out of the sale prior to closing and let the owner keep our good faith money. She offered to let us keep it, as Josh had helped her repaint the house and fix up some things on the inspection list. However, we felt awful as they were a military family and she and her children felt they couldn't join her spouse at his next duty station until they got out from under the house debt they had. So now I had lost my dream of our first home purchase, I had traded in my nice truck for a smaller car to lower the payments, and more and more I just felt like my future was slipping away.

Here is where the worst of the bad advice came in. Well meaning people told us just to file for bankruptcy. So we hired a lawyer and began the process. (Oh by the way, during this time I also found out I was pregnant again. I wanted so badly for this pregnancy and birth to go differently, and it placed an excruciating amount of stress on me.). When all was said and done, we were told we would be able to start rebuilding our credit. Seven years would pass and the bankruptcy would no longer negatively impact our credit score. Well friends, that was in 2004. I sit and write this book in the year 2018, and every credit report I get it is on there. You do the math. What did *not* happen was that we rebuilt our credit. We had only wiped prior debt away, now new bills continued to flood in as we went through a whole new set of diagnosis. We were back to square one with an anchor holding us underwater.

Things I Would Do Differently Today: We should have just kept paying the $5 or whatever we could each month. Medical bills do not affect your credit the way not paying your car payment or your mortgage do. Filing bankruptcy also can mess with your mental state. In talking to some actual reputable financial advisors, I also have learned where to invest our money. For instance, people pushed us to purchase life insurance now that we had a baby. My trusted advisor I now seek advice from taught me that in our situation, long term care insurance makes way more sense; if we were unable to work, we would need income to take care of our family. We set up a will and medical directives, as I mentioned in a previous chapter.

Find financial experts that you can trust. Go to people that actually have financial success and ask who they are using. Just because your family or friends use someone whose personality they like does not necessarily mean that they are doing the best they can to help in financial situations. A good financial advisor will ask questions. They will care about what challenges you have happening in your family. If there is anyone that should have a trusted financial advisor, it is parents who have children with unique abilities and unique medical needs.

You might want to set up a trust for your child. Even if you are overwhelmed with bills and do not think that you have extra income to put aside, it is worth the conversation. A really good financial planner can help assist you in making a budget as well. I am glad that I have someone that I not only know and trust, but someone that I feel good about introducing my friends and loved ones to.

SPOUSE/MARRIAGE

Where do "experts" get their statistics? Sometimes I just want to yell at them. *"DUMB EXPERTS! What do you know anyway?"* Let's take the one about how half of all marriages in the United States now end in divorce. Half? If it's only a fifty-fifty shot that it is even going to work in the first place, those aren't great odds. Imagine you were feeling sick. You have decided to go to your doctor who then tells you your odds are fifty percent either way. I know if a doctor says to me "Well Karen, you've got a fifty-fifty shot of getting through this," even though I know I want to try to go on, and I want to work hard to beat whatever it is... I think I would be seriously contemplating how to finish my bucket list.

When Colton was about to be born, my husband was taken in the hall. The doctor told him that the "odds of survival" were slim. We weren't in a hospital with a major Trauma Center much less a N.I.C.U. Even if the baby was born alive, it would be difficult to stabilize him. Ah...reality check by an expert. I'd love to mail him a graduation notice this spring.

Once our miracle baby did arrive, wailing plenty loud for the world to pay attention to him and peeing all over our pediatrician, he was whisked away from me. As I shared earlier, my husband Josh followed him all the way to St. Louis Children's Hospital that night. When I finally arrived over twenty four hours later, one of the first things they wanted to do was pull us into a N.I.C.U. parent support group. I politely declined. Maybe

I wasn't polite. I honestly don't remember that part. I do remember being in a conference room of some sort with paper brochures galore being pushed at us. Somewhere amid the pile of breastfeeding, what to expect in the N.I.C.U., Physical Therapy, Occupation Therapy, Speech, What to Expect if your Baby has Surgery, etc brochures, it was mentioned that some eighty three percent of marriages with a sick or disabled child end in divorce. *What the heck?* So now my fifty-fifty shot at marriage actually has less than a twenty percent chance? Daaaaang. Commence marriage bucket list.

I can see it. I totally can understand why a marriage could crumble under such circumstances. Parents are absolutely exhausted. Many times, they take shifts taking care of their child so they are separately running errands, working, spending time with other children or even socializing on separate schedules. One parent might decide not to work outside the home because it's easier to be there, and begin to harbor resentment for the one that gets to leave everyday.

The financial strain can cause such an enormous amount of stress. It completely changes what you can and cannot do. For instance, we got a cheaper car, decided to downsize our home, and knew that some of the goals and dreams that we had just honestly may not ever be achieved, or would have to be pushed off to a much later time in life. It was many years before we were first able to travel for a simple family vacation with just our own family, and not have the help or financial assistance of other family members. I could see how, if parents did not put each other as a priority, it could be very hard to maintain a successful relationship.

Even though I am sure the doctors were giving us this data in order to be helpful, I did not appreciate the preconceived notion that we would be one of those statistics. At least, that is how I took it. We looked at each other and kind of rolled our eyes. I think it was just an unspoken promise that we knew we would make it through this journey together.

Josh and I have this thing we do where if we really want to make sure the other accomplishes a task, we say "Do you promise?" It is extremely rare for one of us to say yes to making a promise and then not follow through. We take that word very seriously. To us, our marriage vows were a promise that we made not only with each other, but with God, and our faith is very important to us.

This is the part where I get to brag on Josh, my amazing husband. I cannot imagine what this experience was like for him. Even to this day, I cannot honestly say we have sat down and talked through our feelings. He is a kind-hearted, gentle man (which is probably why he makes such a great Elementary School/Middle School teacher) who is an introvert. I guess opposites do attract, because I could not be more extroverted. So while I am able to share and express how I felt through different phases of our son's life, he tends to hold things in. I'm a self-proclaimed procrastinator, but he is an action taker.

The moment our son was born, Josh jumped into action. He was there standing watch as they stabilized Colton, and he was the one that immediately traveled up to the N.I.C.U. to be with him. When he would come home from football practice each day once Colton returned home from the N.I.C.U., he would quickly change clothes (remember my germophobia?) and come take him from me. He usually would offer to see if I wanted to take a walk or run an errand just so I could get out of the house, which I typically turned down (again, germs) and we would just hang out together. Sometimes we would go over and visit our parents, and we had one other couple that would come to our house for visits. But other than that, our social life was pretty bleak.

Somewhere in that first year, he decided that we needed a getaway. I was absolutely terrified to leave Colton behind. But we did, leaving him in the safe care of my mother, and we went away on just a single overnight trip. It was exactly what I needed. I am happy to say that we have since done an overnight trip every single year. Sometimes it is one night, and sometimes we extended out to two. I know that does not seem like a lot, but we also put our cell phones away and just get to spend quality time together. Matter of fact, on our initial trip to look at homes in Tennessee, we were having so much fun talking with our cell phones put away we accidentally ended up in Indiana! Whoops!

We once took one of those love language quizzes, and I learned that quality time was what my husband wanted the most. It was not that he needed hours upon hours of attention, it was just that when we were together, he needed my undivided attention. We by no means have a perfect marriage, but I do think we have a pretty fabulous one! I believe that some of the keys to success for us have been some of the exact same things that I have mentioned in relationships with other people.

For instance, just like I appreciate when teachers over-communicate with me, I love when my husband tells me something more than once. I would much rather him tell me and I say *"oh that's right, you may have told me that"* than to not know and be frustrated later. Just like dealing with a paraprofessional, he has insights on our children that I do not have. Even though I have my own unique relationship with each of my three kids, so does he. It is so much easier to put our heads together and compare what we have learned, so that together we have more knowledge about each of them. Sometimes people jokingly will ask our kids who is in charge of our house. They all, Josh included, typically laugh and point to me and we all have a good giggle about how I am Queen of the House. They each have been given their Royal titles as well, but later I am always sure to tell the kids, it's Dad and I as partners. They know that there will be no decisions made without us consulting one another.

Another reason that I think our marriage has been successful is that we have always been supportive of each other's goals outside of our marriage. When my husband was offered that first head coaching job he was ecstatic, and I know he wanted to accept it right away. Instead, he always came to me and asked my opinion. I think he would have done it no matter what, but it does make me feel important that he wants to include me in such decisions.

When I have been unhappy in some of my career choices, he has always been a great listener. He does not tell me what he thinks I should do, rather he asks great questions that help me figure out my solution. When I did not want to stay home with our son once he was getting healthier, he was very supportive. He knew that I had enjoyed being out in the workforce and he saw how hard it had been for me as I battled postpartum depression.

It is important that you can find someone to help hold you accountable to taking care of yourself. This is an area that I am not always the strongest in. Josh often times comes home from school and will immediately ask me what I ate that day, because he knows sometimes I get caught up in the excitement of work I am doing and I might skip a meal. We often joke if he was not around I might actually starve to death. He is great about taking over small tasks in the household so that I might work on a bigger project. I try to do the same for him when I know that he has something he is working on. Together, we are teaching our children that they all are an important part of keeping the household running. Everyone has their own chores they need to do and when those don't get done, they are keeping someone else from accomplishing their goals. We are trying to teach them that each person matters and that it is our job as a family to help each other be successful.

I will not go into great detail about my own health journey, other than to say several years ago I was diagnosed with multiple sclerosis. The years that built up to that diagnosis had to have been tremendously hard on him. I had a couple of very serious hospitalizations without getting any clear answers as to what was happening with my health. Just like when he tries to help me work through a situation, or just like when Colton was born, Josh asked a lot of questions. I remember him constantly grilling doctors and asking them question after question trying to find an understanding as to what was happening to his wife. Finally, I was diagnosed after I had a seizure while driving.

A few years ago, Josh was asked to be a main speaker for The Fellowship of Christian Athletes at their annual banquet. There were hundreds of people in the room, and of course I wanted to go and hear what my introverted husband might have to say. He was supposed to share about how his faith had impacted his life and how that played into his role as a Coach at the collegiate level.

By now, I bet you have caught on that I am a crier. It does not take too much for my eyes to start welling up and overflowing with emotion. That evening was no different. I had never heard my husband's account of the car accident and the events that happened after. It was heartbreaking.

Long story short, he had received a phone call from the local police saying that I had been located after having a car accident and while there were EMTs on the scene, they were relaying that I was unresponsive.

Unresponsive. It can mean many things right? What it actually meant to the EMTs was that I was breathing, however they could not get me to an alert state. Somehow to my husband, it meant that I had died. Hearing him tell the story, my heart sank. I had no idea that he had gone through this experience. He went on to tell of how he had to make a phone call to my mother, but luckily soon after a neighbor, whose husband was a police detective, rushed over and let him know that I was indeed still in the land of the living and en route to the emergency room in an ambulance. She offered to stay with the kids, and so he made another phone call back to my mother and they both rushed to the hospital.

That banquet really changed my perception. I knew how I had felt about so many things, but never really truly took the time to think about how they must have felt from my husband's perspective. It has helped me going forward to consider his feelings even more when it comes to decision-making. I think one of the hardest parts of us navigating what Colton's adult life will look like is that we both hold such a unique dream in mind for what he will do. It can be hard because of the experiences and exposures we both had (or did not have) prior to parenthood for us to know what to do next. I do know that no matter what the future holds for us and for Colton, especially as we help him transition into adulthood, I am grateful to be in the less than thirteen percent of marriages that succeed. Together, we are beating the odds.

Things I Would Do Differently Today: Honestly, there is not a lot that I would do differently, other than committing even more time to our marriage relationship. My biggest lesson has been to keep our marriage a priority. It's hard being a parent. It's super hard being a parent of a kiddo with special-needs. We are by no means perfect, but we do have each other's back. We are able to see when the other one is at the breaking point and take over for them. It's both our jobs to do laundry, to cook, and to be personal Uber drivers everywhere our kids need to be. We divide and conquer when it comes to being at school meetings or events the kids have going on at the same time. We have 'date breakfast' almost every Sunday morning while the kids are in their Sunday school at church. We do try to take at least one overnight a year together away from the kids. I know one night a year does not seem like much, but many parents don't get that at all. We try to have our friends over, we sit on the deck and laugh and have good clean fun. You know what they say, laughter really is the best medicine.

SIBLINGS

My biggest regret after having a baby with a disability? It has nothing to do with the care he got from specialists, with not letting anyone into our germ free bubble, or with the fear that I wasn't doing enough as a mother. What I regret the most is waiting so long to have baby number two. I was so overwhelmed with the care of this first one. It seemed that since we had left the N.I.C.U. our lives were still filled with long exhausting two hour drives to specialists. They would see him briefly and then tell us we needed to come back in a couple of weeks. Our home was still constantly filled with traffic in and out from all of the different therapists he was seeing.

How on earth could I add a newborn into that mix? How could I split my time between him and another child? I just was not sure I was ready for that yet. Josh and I talked about it and we finally both agreed not to live in fear of what could happen. We would take preventative measures and get set up with a high risk doctor in advance. We asked a few friends as well as my family doctor for recommendations.

With a plan in place, we were thrilled once we were pregnant again. The doctor recommended that I should come back weekly. I would be given an injection that if successful, should stop me from going into premature labor. While I was not excited about the idea of once again driving four hours for only a few minutes at an appointment, I was somewhat relieved at all the support and validation my new doctor was giving me.

We did multiple ultrasounds and he assured me that everything was going just as planned. I knew in my heart this baby was going to be a girl and was not even surprised when the ultrasound confirmed it for me. The pregnancy progressed and as I neared the 27 week mark something unexpected happened. The doctor had told me that it might be normal to have some feelings of anxiety considering last time, but I did not have anxiety.

I started suffering from depression. Full blown, suffocating, hitting-mute-on-the-life-remote depression. I guess you can call it postpartum, but it really was not because the new baby wasn't even here yet. It seems silly to most, I am sure. It sounds silly to me even. This baby, she was probably going to be born on time. All indications were that she was going to be healthy. Why would I be depressed about having everything go right?

I started thinking of all the baby milestones ahead. She would probably sit up on time, she would be able to communicate with us, and she would walk on time. Normal baby things. I started to feel even more enraged for my son. How unfair! Here he was almost four years old and just starting to walk well with his little AFO leg braces. Would she surpass him physically? Would people ignore him now that there was a "normal" baby around? Or would they ignore her because she would be more self-sufficient? What had we done? Only time would tell.

It is true that Colton was not able to walk well but, amazingly, he was very verbal. He had been diagnosed at age two as hyperlexic, and by age three he was already reading well beyond what Josh and I could comprehend. Many people have heard of dyslexia, which is a processing disorder. Hyperlexia is too, but it is the opposite end of the spectrum to dyslexia. Kids with a hyperlexia diagnosis are fascinated with letters and numbers. When Colton was two, he became obsessed with games shows, particularly Wheel of Fortune. We found that he was solving the puzzles very quickly and would clap his hands and squeal with delight as Vanna spun the lit up letters. As happy as solving puzzles made him, he was devastated when the contestants made a mistake or could not figure out the bonus round. Oh, how he cried and sobbed!

We searched anywhere and everywhere trying to find resources to help us understand this particular diagnosis and finally found a book that explained to us how our son was processing words. We were amazed! Her son was just like ours! We weren't the only ones.

Colton exclaimed in his constant three year old speeches to Josh and I that he was very excited about his new baby sister coming. We were not sure how the grandparents would react to the news of our addition, so I gave him a script to memorize. Yes, at age three I gave my son that could not yet walk a script to read! He was so cute telling his 'Même' how when the baby would come they would be best friends and have so much fun together. He was going to love her so much.

I soon gave birth, despite my fears, to one of the greatest joys of my life: my sweet Thalia. She was absolute perfection. Her older brother, on the other hand, very verbally let us know he had apparently changed his mind. He went from being excited about having a new baby sister best friend to yelling "Bye Bye Baby" and making me a little nervous to ever leave them unsupervised together. He would try to pinch or even bite her. I was astonished! Where was this coming from?

Luckily for me I had a three year old that, while he did not always follow auditory clues, loved to read and had that letter obsession. So I posted signs around the home giving instructions, such as "Colton will only hug baby" or "Colton will come hug Mommy right now." I numbered them, so when I saw him approaching her or being frustrated I could call out "Rule #4" as I handed him a laminated copy of the rules, and he would crawl over to get a hug from me for comfort. It worked really well, and I was grateful for his reading skills.

As Thalia grew, she was meeting her milestones on a pretty average timeframe. Of course with all of her brother's delays, we thought she was some sort of genius-rockstar baby. Thalia was up and crawling by six months and super curious about her brother. He was down at her level, since he was not walking, so his toys and activities were always fair game. This increasingly frustrated Colton even more. All I could do was move her elsewhere and try to relieve his frustrations.

Around this time we met with a psychologist. I was a little concerned about Colton's behaviors towards his sister and wanted to make sure we were creating the best environment possible for both of them. I wasn't expecting the advice we got.

He encouraged us to treat them as twins. Not make Thalia older, but allow Colton to have wins and treat him a bit younger than he actually was. The psychologist said perhaps we had gotten into the habit of doing to much for him, and we needed to push him more (Okay, yes... It is highly possible that he was correct.). Colton was speaking so well and could communicate what he wanted, so we had just done what he asked. We were constantly bringing him toys, food, etc. instead of making him go do it himself. The doctor's advice made complete sense to me. So we decided to experiment with this advice and see what would happen with our new set of "twins" that were actually four years apart.

What we found was, just as the psychologist had predicted, we truly had not been pushing him physically or mentally as much as we could have. I think many parents are guilty of this, no matter if your child is typical in development or not. Sometimes it is easier to recognize what they need and deliver versus that child throwing a fit that you just don't want to deal with. Man oh man. That sister of his pushed all his buttons. We did not separate them or move her away. She was crawling on him, over him, and was able to get to his toys faster than he could. She was always touching him and reaching to see what he had in his hands. Much to his disdain, she was always grabbing and trying to eat his food. Then something peculiar started to happen.

Colton learned to crawl even faster. He was pulling up and placing his toys on the sofa or the coffee table because Thalia was not pulling up quite yet and could not reach it. He quit messing around at meal times and grabbed his food quickly. He learned if he did not get to it sooner, another set of little fingers might grab it away from him. He stopped being so frustrated with her and started to play with her instead. Soon, Thalia was pulling up so they stood together to play with toys. Colton started trying to walk more often without support.

We used to say he was a little lazy. Now we knew it was true. Colton started to realize that he could get somewhere faster, so he started walking faster than her. He soon realized he was taller than her so even standing he could put things out of her reach. Ah, being a "so-called" twin to her definitely helped him switch into the role of big brother.

Because of my fear of taking him outside the home when he was an infant, he had missed out on some pretty important social cues that babies learn from other babies. Even though I was not working full time outside the home when Thalia was young, I was much more involved in toddler groups, taking her to Mommy and Me gymnastics, and creating some social opportunities for her. She played in the dirt more than her brother ever had, and made a mess with food, with paints, or playing with bathtub crayons. Once she reached preschool-age, I enrolled her into preschool at a local daycare just so she could be around other children a few days a week. Around that time I ended up going back to work full time, so it was an easier transition for her to go to daycare the year before she started kindergarten.

Even today as teenagers, they continue to have a unique relationship. Thalia is our child that is very book smart, and even though she is a few grades behind her older brother in school, she is always willing to serve as a tutor to him. She explains things more patiently than I ever could. Teachers have told me a couple of times over the years that when children have said something about him, she is quick to step up and speak out as a fierce protector, which is funny to me as she is as introverted as her father.

It is not surprising that she also serves as a peer mentor in the classroom and helps as an aide for students with disabilities. Last year, she was paired with a nonverbal student. Thalia was beaming with pride near the end of the year when the student learned to make a sound that resembled her name. When I saw the movie "Wonder" this past year, I identified with the mother character so much. I saw so many parallels in my own journey. It really broke my heart to see the sister's journey though, and made me want to talk more with Thalia to see how she has felt.

It was hard to ask her if she felt that we paid enough attention to her. True or not, she validated she did feel we had given her enough individualized attention and that she never felt like she was playing second fiddle to her brother. I know most of Colton's most serious medical problems were happening when she was very young, so perhaps she doesn't even remember. As she got older, and especially when we decided to discuss the possibility of more children, we focused on making sure each child got some one-on-one time with each parent for fun activities. We still focus on individual activities with them to this day.

Five years after Thalia joined our family, we added our third child. We lovingly nicknamed him Tornado... and then quickly upgraded to Hurricane! As a little boy, Hurricane Owen pushed his brother in all kinds of new ways. He was more physical in nature than Thalia was. He wanted his brother to engage not only in physical activities, but play games on the Wii with him. He also had the same curiosity, which sometimes got him into trouble rooting around in his older brother's belongings. I imagine that most families that have such a large age difference can tell similar stories... But that's a whole other can of worms. I'll save that for another book.

Things I Would Do Differently Today: I don't want to say that things didn't work out perfectly for our family. Even though I wished we would not have waited so long to have another baby, if I had gotten over my fears, the baby that came next would not have been my sweet Thalia. She has been perfect for her brother. So perhaps for those of you who are still waiting, my words might help give you the little nudge you need.

Siblings are good for all kids no matter if they have an illness or a disability. They have such a completely different relationship with each other compared to the relationship that they have with us as parents. Siblings are secret keepers and co-conspirators. They are some of the first people to teach us boundaries. They are also some of the first relationships we have (outside of our parents) that teach us unconditional love. I am proud of my kids and they way they stand up for one another. They will be the first to tease or have a quick witted remark when we are the only ones at home, but in the face of an aggressor they become a defender as well as a comforter for each other.

PLAYMATES

Oh, the torture! This was an area that I always used to have mom guilt around. Having playmates seemed agonizing. This is a place I felt like I always struggled in helping Colton. I joined some mommy playgroups, but he never wanted to play age appropriately. When Colton was almost a year old and I was suffering from postpartum depression, my mother pushed me to join a local Women's Club and one of the subgroups was a playgroup. They met at the park every single week or in the winter rotated different people's homes.

For me, these play groups were both the most exciting part of my week and the most depressing. The women in my group were fantastic! I could not wait to go interact with them weekly. They were fun and lighthearted, they told the best stories, and they were very welcoming. Many of them remain my dear friends to this day. I have enjoyed watching their children grow, even from afar as many of us have moved to different places or the children are now graduated and starting adult lives of their own.

The hardest part about going to the playgroup was the fact that Colton was developmentally delayed. Watching cute little babies toddling about, it was hard to hear mothers asking each other things like *"How old is she? Look at her go and only eight months old!"* My child was just beginning to roll over.

Mothers love to give other mothers compliments on their babies. They would talk about how amazing each other's child was, and how great it was that they were hitting these milestones. In the meantime my almost one-year-old was laying flat on his back, showing no interest in other children. Excitement for him included banging two blocks together. It was a hard pill to swallow.

They by no means ever made me feel like he wasn't the sweetest child in the world, but as we say in my business world, comparison is emotional cancer. He did not sit up until he was almost 17 months old, and did not walk very well until he was almost four years old. He was just like his mother, stubborn as heck. He would not use a walker, so the best form of practice we could get was to buy him one of those plastic little grocery carts, put flat weights in the bottom, and then fill it up with plastic fruits and vegetables on top of it so that he could not remove the weights.

We were always lucky in his school years. From early childhood all the way through his senior year, other students have been kind and compassionate to him. I know there were a few kids along the way that had something snide to say. I heard it myself on occasion as well as from my daughter's teachers, but for the most part it has been a good experience for us. I realize that not everyone has this reality, but I also believe that compassion is taught.

Kids today deal with bullying to extremes that we parents never had to deal with. Yet, I also have never seen kids doing and caring more about injustice. This young generation is speaking up, they are taking action, and that tells me someone out there is doing something right as a parent!

It was hard not to be included in many events. We had literally three families whose kids always invited my son to parties in elementary school. I have avoided naming people throughout my book, but this one really stands out to be of significant importance. I want to personally thank Julie, Jennifer, and Jill (hmm...ok, that IS kind of weird they all start with J. I swear I am not making this up!) Their children always included Colton in birthday parties, playdates, and other fun family activities. This was a huge learning opportunity for all our children.

I truly believe that children are born with kind hearts. There are definitely children that are more sensitive than others, and I have experienced the most tender children that truly wear their heart on their sleeve. By turning a blind eye to others that are not like you (be it religion, ethnic background, physical or mental disability, etc.), you as a parent are actually doing your child a major disservice.

I am sure there will be people that will read this, roll their eyes, and say that their child is not prejudiced, their child would never say something mean to someone with a disability, a child of another color, etc. because they themselves do not do that. Then answer me this: If your child is black or latino, when was the last time you took them to interact with a white or asian child, and vice-versa? If your child is able-bodied, when is the last time that you invited over a child with a physical disability to be a playmate? When you see someone with a turban on their head and you are a Christian, does it make you fearful? What do you tell your children about the Civil War or the Civil Rights Movement? Have you ever talked to them about the Holocaust? What about September 11th? Are you leaving it up to their teachers to share historical facts only with them? When you see someone in a store that is in a wheelchair, and your child asks you *"What is the matter with them?"* do you quickly tell them that it is rude to stare and to look away or do you offer an explanation of reasons why they might be in a wheelchair?

I was a recreation major in college. In order to finish one of my courses, we had to choose a disability, then go out in public and play the part for an entire twenty four hours. I was actually excited to take on this project and find out the results. I chose to have an invisible heart disease that would make me need to be in a wheelchair even though I seemingly looked okay.

As I pushed myself in a wheelchair up and down the mall hallway that day, many a youngster would come up to me and asked why I was in it. I cannot remember my statistical data that I turned into my professor, but I want to say over 90% of parents immediately offered me an apology for their blunt or rude child. Most of them quickly grabbed the child's hand and ran off. Whenever I had an opportunity, I would engage in conversation with a child and let them know that my heart was really tired. I explained it made it hard for me to walk up and down the halls without getting out of breath. Lots of them then would identify me with someone they knew and were quick to share a story with me. I heard stories of their friends who had asthma and got out of breath. Some suggested maybe an inhaler would help me. Others gave me sympathetic looks and told me that Grandma or Grandpa had a bad heart and they died. They hoped I did not die soon. They truly meant it.

I'm not sure where along the way we start to lose empathy for others. To me, it seems to be something innate that most of us are born with. People seem to have no trouble asking me what race I am. As a biracial woman I have been asked this question my entire life like it was no big deal. But when people saw my young child toe walking and slapping his hands about, they quickly dropped their eyes to the ground and continued on their way. Children, on the other hand, are fascinated by these behaviors.

One of my dear friends called me one day and said she was hoping I could tell her if she handled a situation correctly. Her son had come home from school and was walking on his toes and slapping his hands up and down. In the autism world, we call this stemming. She immediately asked him why he was doing this. He was quick to share with a smile that he had seen

Colton walking down the hall and observed him slapping away. She shared with her son that it was not nice to make fun of other children and that my child was unable to help himself from these behaviors. He in turn told his mother that he was not making fun of my son, that Colton always seems so happy and cheerful so he thought if he tried it himself he might feel the same way! From the mouth of a babe: Isn't perception a beautiful thing?

I didn't know how much Colton was really missing out on in the playmate world until his little sister came along behind him. I was floored with requests. Play dates, skating rink trips, pool days, sleepovers, the list went on. I realized she was his only real and true playmate. As a young child, he preferred the company of adults anyway. In the beginning it was cute, he was constantly being asked to quote things, sing songs, and share his amazing knowledge of game shows. Over the years, I have decided that I am actually okay with the fact I never conformed to try to force him play with other children.

As mentioned above, he did have a few classmates that would invite him to parties and interact on playdates. But for the most part, he was around my husband's friends and football players. You can learn a lot in a locker room and on the sidelines of sporting events. Chances are he probably heard some explicit language and a slew of other terms I would rather he not learn at such a young age. He also saw the best in human nature.

He saw athletes that supported one another. He saw young men that were happy to give a teammate a chance to run a play at practice, even though that same teammate would never run one in a game. Colton had seen athletes bow their head in prayer together, he saw their excitement when they won and their unity after a tough loss. He learned great social skills from people he enjoyed being with. So far, it has always served him well.

Playmates come in many forms. I think what we all truly want for our children is to make sure that they are surrounding themselves with people who choose to do the right thing. Each of my three children are unique in what gifts they bring to the world, and their playmates are also. I want my children to have friends that are the kind of people that others would consider a role model.

Things I Would Do Differently Today: I am glad that I nurtured friendships for myself in those awkward times, because I needed playmates too! Mamas need that connection. I would like to think today I would be more confident and be okay with my son's failure at parallel play. I would just enjoy him as he was instead of worrying about what other people's children were doing. I know even with my other two children, we can talk to them about how friends might be better than them at certain sports or in different school classes, yet my kids are better than their friends are at certain things as well. Just appreciate the uniqueness that every child brings to the world instead of comparing them.

NUTRITION

Okay, kids, here is where my soapbox moment comes in! I have been a health professional for most of my entire adult life. What we eat *matters*. More so for those whose bodies have extra challenges happening.

Think of a metal toy left out in the rain. What happens? Rust happens, right? That's called oxidation. We have oxidative stress happening inside of us each and every day. It happens because we breathe. It happens because we exercise. It happens more because we are stressed out. When our body is fighting harder because of disease and physical or emotional issues, we produce even more of those little rust spots inside of us. Yikes!

There is a solution in the superhero that I lovingly call the food fairy. Superheroes don't always have to wear a cape, and sometimes they just happen to have sparkly wings. At least, this is how I tried to describe it to my own young children. Guess what the Food Fairy brings to combat all of this rust that is going on inside of them? She brings beautiful colors of the rainbows that are found in all the plants all over the Earth. It cleans all of that rust right off of their insides!

Now, I'm not going to sit here and tell you we eat perfect. I get it. If I would let my husband have an I.V. with straight Mtn Dew, he probably would die a happy man. My own personal biggest threat to healthy eating is someone setting a box of donuts in front of me at a meeting. My younger two love candy, and literally experience pain when we throw out the Halloween stuff after a week.

Colton used to eat what's referred to often as the "beige diet" or the "autism diet." His staples included cheese pizza, macaroni and cheese, frozen waffles (those had better have been the eggo specific brand or else he could tell), and chicken nuggets. You'd be amazed to see what he eats today. Colorful fruits and vegetables. Fermented foods. He even went vegan prior to a major surgery because he knew it would cut down his recovery time.

That journey really began when he was seven years old. It took years and lots of patience. When his diet really began changing, something outstanding happened. His little body started healing. His heart condition resolved. The retinopathy resolved. His G.I. issues resolved.

I do want to mention one of the catalysts for our family eating habits was an awesome product that a physical therapist referred to us, called Juice Plus+. It is just concentrated fruit, vegetable, and berry powders in capsules or gummies. Once we started having our little condensed, George-Jetson-style produce, we noticed that he was more accepting of other colors than just beige. *Gasp!*

So I started being really sneaky. I read a cookbook by Jessica Seinfeld called Deceptively Delicious. I learned how to puree all of our produce and hide it in all types of other foods. I did this in small amounts, where it was almost undetectable. I put pureed carrots into meatloaf, pureed cauliflower into mashed potatoes, even pureed sweet potatoes into a grilled cheese sandwich. The more I added in these pureed fruits and veggies, the more everyone in the family seemed to be craving healthier foods.

I was fascinated. I read articles that shared how we eat many foods based on association with emotions, but I was seeing something different. I was seeing my kids' and husband's taste buds actually *change*.

I learned the crowding method. I didn't have to just rip the band-aid off to get my family's eating habits to make changes. Instead of simply taking away their treats, we had to keep adding in more of the good stuff and then their tastes continued to change even more. Even my canned-green beans-hamburger-helper-meat-and-potatoes hubby was starting to eat the strangest things. I saw him eat bell peppers! And tomatoes! *What was earth was happening?*

What we found was, as we slowly continued adding the good stuff in, the cravings for all the not-so-good stuff slowly dissipated. So we were eating a little better than most, and I was pretty happy with myself. In those early days Josh and I were both coaching high school athletics so bus stops at fast food joints were still happening. At home however, we were eating better than ever.

By the time child number three rolled around, I was starting to experience some pretty rough hormonal shifts. I started entering perimenopause, even though I was only in my early thirties. There is no other way to describe it, ladies. It sucked. I was hot, I was cold, I was sweating like a racehorse after the Kentucky Derby. My energy was zapped. I was not sleeping well.

My doctor thought perhaps my abrupt stop to breastfeeding and weaning Owen was contributing to my hormonal shift. I don't know if it did or not, but I was not about to continue on with that little vampire! He was hurting me! I had breastfed him for a year at that point, so I felt like I had done my duty. I started studying nutrition, looking for a way to get more energy. I went back to school. I got certifications in new areas pertaining to diet and went through a course to be a Certified Health Coach. I was glad that I had.

I will not go into the long stories here because I truly believe there will be more Mama Memoirs to come with these topics, but the following year in 2011, my almost two year old Owen was discovered to be anaphylactically allergic to all forms of tree nuts. This was discovered after I gave him a small piece of a cashew and the reaction caused a scary trip to the emergency room. The next summer, I was diagnosed with Multiple Sclerosis. In the fall of 2013, my daughter was diagnosed with a severe case of Crohn's disease. I was dumbfounded. We were eating better than most, yet these things were happening to us. I thought that by changing our diets I was supposed to be helping us get healthier, not get worse.

I dove into every Gold Standard Research Study I could find. I read every article I could about the link between nutrition and disease. If there was a speaker coming to town, be it doctor, nurse, homeopathic, or herbalist, I attended. I took pages and pages of notes. Turns out, I was doing the right thing changing my family's eating habits. The issue lie not in what I was currently doing, but in things that had been happening for years (especially with me) and it just finally had caught up to us.

After a relapse in 2017, I made the difficult choice to start a medication regimen. I am involved in social media chat rooms and support groups where I see people leading a much different lifestyle than mine. I am happy to tell you I live symptom free. The same is true for my daughter, who went from over 120 doses of medication at diagnosis to complete remission today. An active cheerleader and competitive dancer, she has never missed a practice due to injury or illness. Most with autoimmune disease like us can not say this.

What helped me teach my kids to eat differently? The steps I mentioned before, for sure. Adding things in slowly and not making massive changes all at once was a big part. But just as important, I was willing to help them learn about fueling their bodies well for the daily activities they have.

We talk about eating a traffic light system. Green are those great foods they do not ever have to ask permission to eat. They know they can grab fruit out of the basket that I have, or dive into the refrigerator for any chopped and prepared produce. They do have to ask for the yellow light foods. Yellow includes things such as chips, popcorn, and snack bars that they are allowed to have on a limited basis. They are not terrible for them, yet they may not offer the best nutritional support that would help them dance, play sports, or do well in school. The red light category is our treat category. For some, this is their category of things not to eat at all. Our family adapted it to be foods that we might find at a birthday party or at our sporting events. These are not foods that we eat on a regular basis, but I also believe my kids get them so rarely that when they do have them, they don't want anything in large quantities. These might include items like cake, ice cream, sodas, or those donuts I mentioned earlier. They typically will tell us they cannot finish whatever treat they have.

Things I Would Do Differently Today: I am proud of the nutritional research that I did. I do not believe that any and all disease can be cured with nutrition alone. Other factors play in for sure. Stress, exercise, hydration, and sleep are just a few. I think anyone that would say otherwise is opening themselves up to tremendous liability. I can say that, in my opinion, there is no condition that can not at least benefit from improved nutrition. I think what I would do differently today is be more open minded to the concept that certain foods are just not supporting my family's health, no matter how convenient they are. I think today I would place more value on being healthy and fueling our bodies for success instead of dieting to look a certain way. I would want to be more open that even small nutritional changes

can have a significant impact. I would most certainly be bolder in sharing my mission to help bring families back to the dinner table together. Creating a healthier nutrition plan can add years back into our lives and give us more time with the people we love and cherish.

TRAVEL

Traveling. Ugh. Where do I even start? I think I got my first dose of true travel reality when I accompanied my in-laws on a beach vacation. Colton was six at the time and Thalia was only two. Neither was potty trained. That's right. I said that neither one was potty trained. On a beach. All day. Every day. For a week. With a 6 year old and a 2 year old. With two little people who, for whatever reason, couldn't appreciate that putting their poop in the potty would make vacation and life in general so much easier for Mommy.

Josh had just started a brand new job as a collegiate football coach, so he decided that he really shouldn't travel on this trip with us. *Important Tip: Do not travel without support. Lots of support.* Let's just say that my dreams of yoga on the beach at sunrise were never achieved. Add in the fact that it was a two-day drive each way and little Miss was always puking from being car sick... You can imagine how quickly I resigned to the fact that staycations with tents in the living room must be the best way ever invented to vacay.

It's not just traveling for major vacations that can be difficult. My perception has been that difficulties can lie with all outings in general. Everywhere. Heading to the grocery store, a park, eating out at a restaurant, going to the movies, or even just going over to a friend's home for a cookout/family gathering. It was overwhelming worrying about if there would be sick people around us. Would Colton be upset by some visual or auditory stimulation? I know that our child does not have the severity in his disabilities as some of you reading this, so I cannot image the overwhelming feelings you must have when it comes to running errands or traveling. For me, it felt like when we went out to eat, people stared at us. I know that people made comments. It stings. It becomes easier to stay in. But Mamas...don't.

Sometimes it is absolutely necessary for you to stay in, that is not what I am speaking about. Some children can not be exposed, especially during the winter months. Their immune systems are just too compromised. Then there are some children who literally need an entire van full of equipment just to leave the house. That is not what I mean either. I have friends in that exact situation and I wish I could change things and make it easier for them.

Even though I could simply put my child in a car and leave, I just chose not to on many occasions. Don't be trapped by the lie that it's too much effort to pack up or because fear is stopping you from overcoming challenges. All children need experiences. We, as the parents, needed more experiences. The more we went on outings and the more our little man experienced, the more changes we saw in our child. He seemed more interested in anything and everything. The new sights and sounds created new exploration. Before he might be content to sit at home and spin the same toy car... did you know that matchbox cars spin really well if placed upside down? (If you're a mom with a kiddo on the Autism Spectrum, yeah, you probably already knew that).

In Colton's younger years, a new classroom was a complete visual overload. We would try to meet with the teacher a couple weeks before school even began. We wanted Colton to tour the classroom or play in it prior to the school year starting so that he could get used to the posters and billboards full of fun colors, shapes, and textures. As he got older and we started traveling more and more, the exploration he was having was paying off. We truly did see increasingly less visual distraction happening.

Something unique happens to all of us when we travel, not just to a kiddo like mine. Do you ever drive the same route over and over? Maybe it is taking your kids to school or going to the grocery store. You are there all of the sudden, but you can not say for sure you actually remember driving there. Then there is a route change due to construction or you have to run a different errand after you drop the kids off, and you are just amazed by the beautiful homes you passed or a blooming tree. You wonder, *"Has that always been there?"* You are traveling! Your mind is waking up.

Colton used to scream and cry hysterically at buzzers (trust me, this really sucks when your dad coaches basketball), yet now I am always teasing him that he should become a color commentator for how he yells during any sporting event he watches on television. Colton is a huge Tennessee Titans football fan and enjoys going to watch them play with his Dad. He loves traveling back to Missouri to see his beloved St. Louis Cardinals. We used to have to put noise cancelling earphones on him for all these functions. Even the bells being rung at Sunday Mass would cause an upset.

Slowly, as we continued to put him into these situations with love and support, he became better adjusted. He just needed to learn to navigate through the noise. Will this work for all children that have sensory issues? I do not imagine that it would. I wish that there was a simple solution for everyone. All I can share is what worked for us. Just like with us, it takes many repetitions for anything to become a habit. For Colton, each repetition helped him settle in a little bit more. It was not easy. People still stared and made comments, but because we were willing to be patient and let him work through it, we eventually made it to the light on the other side of that tunnel!

Josh loves cooking breakfast! I don't mean he likes pouring cereal. I mean, this man loves flipping pancakes and making omelets for people. He always said we should start a bed and breakfast because I love to entertain and he can make breakfast. However, we also love to travel and did not want to be tied down owning a hands on business like that. So the dream got put off to the side and we tried to decide how could we best serve people who have struggles like us. Obviously the biggest pulls to our heart strings are for people like our son who have unique abilities.The gifts they shine into the world are truly amazing, however for them going on a fun adventure, trying to have recreational activities, or travel can be a challenge. We had a dream in our hearts to start a foundation to address a couple of the major pitfalls that we found for traveling and recreation: cost and access.

Our hometown back in Missouri did not really have anything at all for our son. He was not able to be included in soccer or t-ball. We paid for private gymnastics so he could try something. He did swim lessons well, but that was about it.

We made the move to Tennessee when he was in middle school. We were thrilled to find so many amazing resources here. One is a wonderful program called Buddy Ball. He loves, and is able to participate in, multiple kinds of activities throughout the year. He plays basketball, he has done water polo, he dubbed himself Mister September during baseball season, and he goes bowling. They truly create a wonderful environment for the kids and any siblings that want to participate. We wanted to create an opportunity for all people to feel included this way.

We also found that many "Handicapped Accessible Parks" are pretty poor at inclusion. For instance, we toured a park that had wood chips as the surface material. This would provide a soft landing for a fall for sure, however for someone with very unstable balance (like Colton), this would actually be more likely to cause the fall in the first place. As we travel, we find that places are usually considered 'accessible' if they simply have a ramp present. We want to shine a light on the difference between things being accessible and things being inclusive. Inclusive means that anyone and everyone can participate.

Our goal with our Colton's Corner Foundation is first and foremost to inform others of places (recreational activities, parks, etc) that we find to be truly inclusive, and to give those places our "seal of approval," so to speak. Secondly, we aim to start raising funds in order to add in recreation equipment to existing structures that make them more inclusive. It is more cost effective to add to what's already there than to start from scratch over and over.

We also want to eventually provide respite care funding for parents who typically are not able to travel as a family. Having a trained RN or similar medical professional along is very expensive. These funds could allow a family to experience a new piece of the world together, something they likely never expected to do.

Things I Would Do Differently Today: I would have stayed in uncomfortable situations longer and let my child figure out what he needed. It is not my problem, nor the problem of children and parents just like our family, to worry about the uncomfortable feelings that others have. They are simply uneducated about what we are going through or dealing with. They may see our child's stemming or tantrum and think we are just dealing with a misbehaving child. Too many of us shut ourselves away to avoid such confrontation. Today, I would always put my child first and help him learn about the

environment he is in, allowing more people to be exposed to behaviours like his and learn about children like him.

I.E.P. MEETINGS

The dreaded I.E.P. meeting. Having a child spend three years in an early childhood program, then kindergarten and twelve years of school equals no less than sixteen I.E.P. meetings. This does not even count the times that we went in to make changes, reading over drafts that were mailed to us, etc. Most of these meetings I attended on my own. As years passed and my confidence grew, I felt like a prize fighter entering the ring. Boxing gloves up, ready position, and there was no way that anyone was going to take me down! I've got the eye of the tiger!

It might sound dramatic, but as an educator's wife, I've learned that most teachers equate attending an I.E.P. meeting to going to the dentist to get a tooth extracted. There is literally nothing they can do to avoid it, it is just one of those things that they have to suffer through. Teachers, am I lying here? It has nothing to do with the level of care they have for the child, it's just a part of the educational process no one enjoys.

Some of you may be a bit lost. An I.E.P. is an Individualized Educational Program. It is a written statement for a child that, in theory, will help carry out their unique learning styles and help parents, staff, and the student work together to create success in the classroom.

Notice, I said in theory. I have yet to meet a parent that tells me how happy they are because the I.E.P. that has been written for their student is creative genius. The I.E.P. is supposed to take into account your child's strengths and their talents, however those strengths and talents are often overlooked. Many times, goals are just set because that is what is easier for the educational system to track. Round peg, round hole.

I especially think of elementary school teachers. They dream of the colorful billboards they can decorate their classrooms with, the cute little activities they can do with their students, and what their students will grow up to be. This is why most of them got into teaching. I doubt too many teachers sat in colleges and universities across the country and thought to themselves, *"Boy I sure cannot wait to be invited to my first IEP meeting. I bet that will be the highlight of my teaching experience!"* The teachers are being pulled out of the classroom or their planning periods, the administrators are being pulled away from their long list of To Do's, and even for parents, it just is not something to look forward to.

Some students also have what is called a Section 504. This is more health-related. For instance, my daughter has a 504 because of Crohn's disease. Therefore, she is flagged in the system, and teachers know that she is allowed to excuse herself from the classroom without penalty. A 504 is typically less restrictive than an IEP.

There are also differences between educational diagnosis and medical diagnosis. Let's take autism for instance, because this is a challenge that more and more parents are having to deal with. Autism is one of the fourteen categories recognized by the Individuals with Disabilities Education Act. However, even if your child has a medically recognized diagnosis given in a clinical setting by a medical professional, that does not necessarily mean the school will recognize the same need for services.

Do not worry, I can't imagine a public school setting where services would not be provided to assist a medically diagnosed child. However, the range and spectrum of services provided could be where differences of opinion will occur. For instance, our son received speech therapy services all the way until high school. I still believe he could benefit from speech therapy, however it just was not worth the impact of pulling him out of the classroom any longer. It is important to discuss both an I.E.P. and a 504 option within your family. Although the school will have a recommendation, and a trusted medical professional can have an opinion as well, it ultimately boils down to your family and what you believe will be the best way of supporting your child in their academic career.

I implore parents not to get trapped in the worry of their child being "labeled." Some of the world's most creative geniuses had some form of a "label" as a child. Instead, I choose to think of our I.E.P. as a tool to make sure my child is getting not only the services he needs to be successful in his education, but that he is legally being treated and supported in a learning style that works for him. Without that I.E.P. he would not have extra time on tests, preferential seating in the classroom, or be able to retake/rework certain assignments and quizzes he did not perform at a certain standard on. It has been a critical part of his success.

The National Center for Education Statistics (http://nces.ed.gov) website states that in 2015–16, the number of students ages 3-21 receiving special education services was 6.7 million. That's *thirteen percent* of all public school students. Among students receiving special education services, thirty-four percent had specific learning disabilities. Thirteen percent is a definite minority amongst students, yet for each of those students, there is so much planning that goes creating opportunities for them to be successful in the school setting.

The first year that my son was enrolled in early childhood, I had no idea what an I.E.P. meeting even was. I sat back and listened as one of his therapists read pages and pages of goals for the following year. He would have to jump with both feet at the same time and come an inch off the ground. He would have to hold a ball in one hand and toss it across the room to her. He would recognize facial expressions and understand basic language. These all seemed pretty simple, as did their system for recognizing if the goals were met. Some of his goals he had completed at eighty percent accuracy. Sounds pretty good to me, I thought.

It was hard to know what we should expect for our child, especially at a young age. What is the significance of throwing a ball with one hand, and how that will equate to what he can do as a high school senior? Did being able to jump one inch off the ground with both feet mean that he was going to be able to walk at his high school graduation? Dance at prom? Or was it just so that he would be able to get off the curb without tripping? All of the sudden, these thoughts started swirling around in my brain. How would I ever figure this out? Did they understand the goals they were setting and how they would affect my child in the long run?

One thing that I have learned over the years is to set the end goal first. That was not something that I had done with Colton. I was consumed by the overwhelming day-to-day of schooling, caring for his newborn sister, and navigating constant medical trips and home appointments. Now we had added in a public school program where he was receiving multiple therapies as well.

If I could go back in time, I definitely would want to think ahead and dream bigger for my child. This is one thing I recommend parents doing. Even though things might seem frustrating and perhaps even hopeless, depending on the stage you are in with your child, try to imagine five, ten, even twenty years from now... What is the end goal?

As an educator, Josh has been pulled into many I.E.P. meetings. One particular meeting stands out. The student was not a student of his, however the educators and the parents were having trouble connecting. They thought since Josh had a child on the autism spectrum, he might be able to relate to this mom on a parent level. When he went into the meeting, he could sense her frustration as they talked about percentages of goals met. Was her child meeting the math goal at the eightieth percentile? Was her child able to cognitively comprehend the word problems that they had been working on in math class? Was she as the parent aware of missing assignments and what did she feel his goals should be in the classroom? My husband stepped in and gave her emotional and social goals to set for her child.

He asked her *"Have you ever thought about what he's going to do when he grows up? What is it that you would like to see for your child? Let me give you an example that my wife and I have set for our son. We want him to interact with his peers at school properly. We want for him to come out of high school and be able to take advantage of enrolling in a university setting if he wants to, but also taking only a college course if he is interested. Our most profound hope is that he becomes a functioning member of society. Have you thought about goals like this?"*

The mother broke down in tears. No one had ever asked her about her hopes and dreams for her son. No one had ever asked her what it is that she hoped he would be able to do not only after middle school, but after high school. Unfortunately the I.E.P. setting truly is about what they are doing in the moment. Remember that, parents. Think ahead to what you want for your child and know that you can help structure that I.E.P. to help set them up for success. If my son gets a "C" in algebra class, is that going to keep him from living his best life ever? Hardly.

Instead, I believe the experiences he is having as a high school student will help shape him into the person he is going to be. Going shirtless on a Friday night at a football game covered in body paint, chanting loudly with his peers on the sidelines to cheer on his friends, sitting in the lunchroom where his mother has told him to stay off his technology and instead engage in conversation with his peers, and worrying about who he might ask to the upcoming dance; these are actions that cannot receive a score on an I.E.P. meeting printout. But they are significant in nature because they are teaching him how to *actually function and interact* as a member of society.

Going back to that early childhood setting, we reached the end of the program and we were told that we now will prepare to transfer our son into kindergarten. Whew, we made it. What an exciting bridge! Actually, that is what they called the I.E.P. meeting that setting. It was going to be a bridge meeting, because for this meeting there would be a representative there from any and every class, program, or therapy that my son would come into contact with, as well as the ones from the previous year. That meant there would be two speech therapists, two physical therapists, two occupational therapists, two physical education teachers, and his Early Education teacher as well as next year's potential kindergarten teacher. It kind of sounds like Noah's Ark doesn't it? Here they came two by two. I got to thinking, that sure sounds like a lot of people sitting around this table and the only person that is here to advocate on the part of my child is me. Although teachers will say that they are there to advocate for your child, please remember that they are there to advocate for the school system. Their job is to follow the policies that have been set forth by their administration.

I reached out to a few friends, and a girlfriend that worked for the state in special education said she would be happy to attend this meeting with me. With her and my mother coming, I was just happy that there would be two people in my corner of the boxing ring, while the school would seemingly have ten or more. Her support turned out to be such a huge blessing. This was not my first I.E.P. meeting, however it was the most formal I.E.P. meeting we had ever had.

As one therapist began to read through the pages and pages of documents, like we had in years past, my friend constantly stopped her and made corrections. She told the therapist that she was not reading the document as written, and they all seemed quite taken aback. You could see their eyes widening and the looks of surprise as they looked around at each other. It's not that their casual approach had bothered me at all, I was quite happy to get through it in record time, however my girlfriend taught me that this is a legal document and should be treated as such.

I started to equate it to purchasing a home. I would not sweep through the contract quickly and say, "Yeah, yeah, I'm sure it's fine." I want to go over it with a fine-tooth comb with a realtor. A realtor's job is to know the language and to make sure that what is being presented in front of me is actually in my best interest.

An I.E.P. meeting is no different. There are so many people that can go with you and be an advocate for you and your child. You can hire professionals (many outside therapists do charge an hourly rate), or there are state agencies that are happy to send an advocate with you for free. I recommend doing both, especially in the early years. There is nothing wrong with making sure that everything on that document is in your child's best interest.

If you do not like something, speak up. This is where other mothers can come in. If your child does not have an outside advocate or a therapist willing to come in and sit in your corner, ask a friend. You have a right to have anyone there that you believe can speak about your child. Perhaps it's a close family friend, perhaps it's someone from your church, perhaps it's a grandparent. Even if they do not speak during the meeting, I promise you that your own composure will be so much better knowing that someone is there to emotionally support you.

Looking back, I wish that I had done this more often. Not only can those year-to-year I.E.P. meetings feel overwhelming, the transitional years (when you jump from elementary to middle school to high school) are brutal. We had an unfortunate experience, resulting in deciding to pull him out of the regular classroom and end his last year of elementary with homebound instruction. In the next chapter of this book, I will write about teachers. You will hear me say that I never pulled my child out of any classrooms in order to make a situation easier for him. The reason he was pulled out this time was not due to the teacher whatsoever, it was due to a safety concern.

For this particular transitional meeting, the analogy about going to the dentist no longer fits. At this point, the only analogy that properly demonstrates my feelings is waterboarding, or perhaps one of those old style torture methods where they lay you down and strap your arms and legs and then horses pull your arms and legs in four separate directions until you snap. Drawn and quartered. Pure agony.

We had just gone through pulling him from school after a safety-related scare. Plus, this was one of those meetings that was like Noah's Ark. Josh and I tackled this one together.

The best part of the meeting was when the original elementary team left. The teachers and staff he would deal with in middle school basically let us wipe the slate clean and come into their school with no set expectations on either side. It changed the trajectory of his education. They were kind and patient. This is likely why the children that interacted with him were also kind and patient. They were given wonderful examples of how to treat others.

They even had a day each year where parents and kids that had unique abilities or chronic illness were given an opportunity to speak to their peers. Class after class came through for short sessions with us to bluntly ask questions about my son and his disabilities. As I mentioned before, children are only curious and want to learn. If you give them an explanation they can understand, they are quite willing to accept it. My son just adored his middle school principal, whom he fondly nicknamed his Steel Magnolia, and his vice-principal who made him feel like he was the coolest cat walking the school. He has had so many amazing teachers, aides, and counselors that poured into him over the years that I wish I could recognize each and every one. Going to the dentist, nor an I.E.P. meeting, doesn't have to be a painful experience.

Things I Would Do Differently Today: I've said it before, and I'll say it again: a good support system goes a long way. I wish I had had at least one person, if not more, to attend every I.E.P. meeting with me. I have been privileged enough to have gone in and sat in the corner for some of my friends and family members. Having someone on your side shifts the energy of the room. It shows the I.E.P. team that you are taking an active approach in your child's education. You get to set the tone and make sure that the expectations you want are heard.

Reach out in parent groups. Instead of asking for opinions from parents complaining about how the meeting went, seek out parents that feel they have learned the system well and know how to navigate it over the years. A parent of an older child can be a huge resource. They can help you stay calm and pick your battles, or nudge you to ask for more in order to support your child.

Remember, it's not you against the system. Rather, learn how to advocate for your child to ensure that your child comes out of school as their best possible self.

TEACHERS

I already talked about I.E.P. meetings, so I might as well jump right into teachers. Teachers: the good, the bad, and the ugly. Okay, none of them are ugly. They are all beautiful human beings for going into such a giving profession. Most of them spend more time with other people's children than they do with their own. Throughout my marriage with Josh, I've experienced this in person!

These are people that are overworked and underpaid. Yet, the little money they make is often reinvested back into their students. They purchase classroom items to make your child's education more fun. Behind the scenes, they are doing things like making sure kids have enough food by handing out snacks for the entire classroom so it will not be so obvious. Sometimes it goes even further than that. Perhaps they are sending groceries home in backpacks to make sure the child has something to eat over the weekend. Sometimes they go together to make sure a child has a warm coat for winter or a pair of mittens. When I was younger, a local group of teachers purchased a suit so a student could attend a school dance. I really can not give a more glowing testimonial to the heart of most teachers and the lengths they are willing to go to help your child be a success.

The thing I will say about teachers, however amazing and wonderful they are, is that you know your kiddo better than they do, no matter what they may believe. I've had teachers over the years tell me as much. *"Mrs. Richards, I think I know a little more about Colton and (insert whatever they might say) than you do…"*

Well, let me put my hand up right there. While I agree that there are teachers who had a bird's-eye view to my son's unique learning style and behaviors, they still didn't have my view. The view of the one person that continually hopes and dreams for this child. The one that cried ugly tears (and still does) when a kiddo like mine accomplished a task others take for granted. At the end of every school day, that teacher gets to go home to his or her own family.

Over the course of my son's education, a teacher gets an incredible nine and a half months to leave their stamp on his life. In the blink of an eye, it is over. They have the power to make me love them tremendously, or as I have learned, to be tremendously grateful for the lessons that I learned because of them.

I never once took *any* of my three children out of a class because I "heard something about that teacher". Guess what, Mamas? The world can be *mean*. The world isn't *flexible*. As much as we want the life of our kids to be masterfully crafted, a fairytale filled with unicorns and magic, we do them a much greater service by preparing them for their life ahead. They are going to need more than having the nicest and most popular teacher each year. I would much rather have someone teaching my child that is firm and that will discipline them while still having compassion. Someone who teaches empathy, rather than someone who is considered nice.

I have often appreciated teachers that are very good at communication. I truly believe that good communication is the key to helping unlock your students' unique potential. I have always made sure to meet my children's teachers face-to-face. I show up for meet the teacher nights and school conferences. When I offer to come into the classroom and do something, I mean it! Especially at the elementary level, and even with typically learning children, simply making copies or cutting out objects for teachers makes a huge difference.

The demand being placed on teachers is greater than ever. Many of us complain about test scores and the politics that have come into education, but that is not your child's teacher's fault. They are also trying to navigate through it the best that they can, knowing that they themselves are being graded by state testing results.

With Colton, it was important to communicate as much as possible with his teachers. Sometimes it was as simple as a notebook that he carried with him. The teacher might jot down events that happened during the day or share if he had needed extra time on a test. In turn, I could write a short note to let them know if he had been upset at home by anything that might create challenges for the teacher at school. They always seemed to appreciate this as much as I did. Be sure and talk to your child's teachers and find a communication system that works. It is much easier to proactively over-communicate than it is to try to reactively change things you didn't see coming.

There is definitely a hierarchy that exists in the school system. We actively tried to never to jump over anyone and go up the chain of command. However, there are times that you need to have someone come in and intercede. For instance, if you have communicated to a teacher and have not gotten a response, or you do not feel the I.E.P. is properly being followed, then it would be appropriate to call in to either your I.E.P. coordinator or your school administrator to try to set up a meeting.

There were times in the past that we were not happy with the answer that we received, so we continued to go up the chain of command. Many times we met with a school principal. There were times it went all the way up to a superintendent. I cannot say that we were always happy with the outcomes, however I am happy that we at least tried. If you reach the top of the hierarchy and they are not even aware that things are happening, it means that no one is complaining, no one is challenging things that are wrong, and no one is speaking up. You will never make changes for your child by complaining on social media or to your friends. Again, I remind you that YOU are the most important advocate for your child.

This is where it is important to continue the proactive communication with people in the school building. Are you going in and volunteering on a regular basis? Perhaps if you work outside the home this is not possible, but maybe it is possible for you to take a shift for an event like a school carnival or a book fair that happens outside of school hours. Knowing the people that are coming into contact with your child is an important step. When they get to interact with you and see your concern or your excitement for your child's learning, it spills over onto them. As they get to know you and your child better, they are willing to be key players in your child's success. Perhaps it is your school librarian or the physical education teacher. Perhaps it is the art or music teacher that will be able to reach your child. Even though these are are areas that are not going to be listed for goals on the I.E.P. documents, these are educators that can be great resources.

The school librarian, for instance, might be able to recommend some great noise cancelling earphones or give your child's teacher new resources. They also can give you different tips and places to find educational tools outside of school. The physical education teacher has likely had to take classes themselves in order to find activities for your child to do. Some of my son's former physical education teachers have been able to point me to books and other resources for recreational activity. It is almost common knowledge that music works wonders with stimulating the brain, and a music teacher might be able to tell you the types of music they have seen that grabs your student's interest. Perhaps playing such music while your child is working on their homework could be helpful. On the other hand, it's very helpful to know what types of music create the most distraction for your child.

Another tip I can share is that paraprofessionals, just like those amazing N.I.C.U. nurses, can be your greatest ally. They have the inside scoop to teachers and the school system without having the extra demands the teacher has (lesson plans, going to the I.E.P. meetings, and dealing with the politics of the school district). Find out who your school, classroom, and student paraprofessionals are and create a relationship with them.

These are people that typically do not have the full educational degree that teachers have, or they are awaiting an open position elsewhere in the school district. They are being paid much less than the teachers, and sometimes work more one-on-one with the students that actually need the extra help. They will be able to tell you more about your child's classroom setting than anyone else. These are the people that are in the trenches with your child.

They might be able to tell you if your child is having certain triggers in the classroom, if they are succeeding in one area more, or anything else they might have noticed. Even when it comes to health issues, even though they are not medical professionals, they spend a lot of time with your child. They can be one of the people that can assess when your child is at their baseline. If your child is not feeling well, they might be one of the first people to notice. This is especially important for children that are nonverbal and may not be able to tell you what they are feeling.

Teachers have tremendous power and influence shaping your child's education, from early childhood until they are an adult. From Colton, who needed support in all areas, to Thalia, who seemed to need none, to Owen that has needed some support in his reading, Josh and I have learned the importance of forging relationships with their teachers and other educators in their buildings. A good relationship goes a long way into creating success for your student.

Things I Would Do Differently Today: This is a hard one. I do not know that I would do a lot differently here, other than really try to get into relationships with as many of Colton's teachers and support staff as I could. It definitely made it much easier over the years. Why would you never have face-to-face time with the people that are educating your children? Especially in the elementary years, their teachers may see them more in the weekdays than you do!

I also wish I had worked harder to find more opportunities for Colton to have recreational experiences when he was younger. If I had realized the lack of options, even in the school setting, I believe I would have taken a more active interest in my community and been proactive in bringing more opportunities for children like Colton.

TAKING CARE OF THE CAREGIVER

Author Rachel Hollis has a vase analogy that I really love. In her *Made for More* documentary, Hollis talks about how sometimes, as women, we take everything that is being poured into us and we feel the need to pour it out to others. We pour it out to our children, to our spouse, we pour it out to our friends, our church community, and our school community. She shares how the problem is we continue to tip and pour out until finally the glass vase that is our self, shatters. She said to imagine instead that the strong vase stands upward and all the goodness that is being poured into us continues until it reaches a point that it's simply overflows to those around us.

I definitely have tipped over and shattered time and time again. I see the shards of glass that were my former self lying on the floor. I see so many small fragments that I am not sure can ever be put together again. Instead, maybe it would be easier to come along with a broom and dustpan to just dump all these fragments into the trash. I imagine lots of mothers feel that way. I imagine even more parents feel that way when they have a child with a medical diagnosis that is draining them emotionally, physically, and financially.

As I have mentioned earlier, it is said that parents who raise children with intense needs are far more likely to have marital issues. It has been shown through many studies that the consequences of chronic stress also lead to higher numbers of parents living through anxiety, depression, fatigue, and insomnia.

Parents raising children with a disability are more likely to suffer feelings of isolation. As parents, it is hard not to reach the point of burnout because we fail to set a limit for ourselves on the amount of items that we can accomplish.

I wish I could tell you that I've always taken really great care of myself. However, it's been a learning process. As a fitness professional, I did eat better than the average joe, and I was exercising on a regular basis. This probably served me in Colton's younger years better than anything else that I was doing. I have fallen off and on the exercise train in recent years. It happens. You just gotta find something you love and jump back on that train!

One thing that has helped me was learning to become a time blocker. This activity has not only served me well in my business life, but it has also served me well in my personal life. While blocking time might sound like wishful thinking to parents frazzled by a busy kid's calendar, I assure you it is helpful. Whether you have a sick family member or not, time blocking can help your household run so much more efficiently. Time blocking is an important part of self care.

For instance, I tend to have several video conferences and phone calls every Monday. Therefore, Monday is not a day that I typically allow any kinds of appointments to be scheduled outside my home. No dentist, no doctor checkups, no lunch dates, or girl time. This is the day that I get to stay in my yoga pants and get things done. Josh and the kids are back to school, and the house becomes mine again. Even though I work from home, I still have a lengthy list of things that need to get done each week. The piles in my office look like towers sometimes. While I might run out for a quick morning yoga class, I am home most of the day.

Monday is my cooking day. I'm a meal prep fanatic. I like to plan out my menu and go to the store on Sunday for anything missing from my ingredient list. I do the bulk of my shopping once a month to grab my staples: spices and seasonings, spaghetti sauce, soup bases, pasta, or frozen vegetables. This four week cycle works well to make sure that when I run to the grocery on Sundays, I do not get overwhelmed with a long list. Mainly, I go for produce and potentially a couple other items. Back to the menu. After I've written out my menu, I get to cooking! I might have all four of my stove top burners going, as well as both ovens and my instant pot. Sundays when I get back from the grocery store, I will cut up, dice, and prepare any of the fresh fruits and vegetables that I got and put them in clear containers in the refrigerator. That way when it comes to preparing meals throughout the week it is easy to just grab a few things here and there and *voilà*! Dinner is served.

Having an emergency plan has helped me to take better care of myself because it keeps my stress level down. It may sound like an odd thing to do, but I made sure that my electric company and water company knew that I had a handicapped child in the home. Times when there were power outages, water line issues, or other emergencies, that puts us on a priority list to have things restored. I always keep just a couple gallons of bottled water around. We also keep a dry erase board near the telephone so that babysitters or grandparents would have a list of people to call if something came up.

Having what I call daily "Me Time" is also important. Some people like to get up about 15-20 mins early to read devotionals or the Bible. Sometimes that works for me, sometimes it does not. Sometimes it's really hard to have faith. It might be your faith has taken a flying leap out the window. For me, faith has been a great comfort. There have also been times I just am living in my own world of ungratefulness and not giving the glory where it is due. Faith can come from many different places. It can be in people that are just there to recognize and support you, even if you have different religious beliefs. I have a book club that I recently have been meeting with online. It's an amazing group of women that make me laugh and offer community. That has been a wonderful Me Time activity.

Even if it is just taking a bath after the kids go to bed at night, having a little time to yourself somewhere in the day is so important for your mental health. Especially now that we are all tied to technology, we need that time for our brain to shut off. People think that I am nuts when I tell them we only have one television in the house, but it is part of my plan to keep us from distraction. Watching television is something that we can all come out in the living room and enjoy together as a family. I have trained our brains so that when we enter our bedrooms, our bodies start to recognize it is time to unwind and shut down. My children and I typically do not have a problem falling asleep because of this. It is really important to have routine in order to get into a relaxed state. Breathing exercises also have helped when I or my children are having trouble sleeping. I get them to take a deep inhale through their nose, hold their breath for just a moment, and then slowly let the air out, much like you would do in yoga class.

Therapy is another form of self care. As human beings, we crave connection with others. Sometimes it helps to be able to open up and share our experiences. Find a trusted friend or adviser you can share your struggles with. However, finding a licensed professional can also help you dive in even deeper to the emotions that you are feeling. Professional therapists are able to lead you through exercises and bring out things that we may feel ashamed to confide in our friends. Even though we might share some of what we are feeling with loved ones, most of the time we still hold back sharing everything.

I know for me, there is a lot of guilt that I am still trying to navigate through. You might wonder, what on earth do I have to feel guilty about? I really do not know. Perhaps it is the feeling of guilt that I missed something. Perhaps it's thinking I didn't dedicate enough time to one child or the other at any given moment. Perhaps it was fear that I may have done something to cause my child to be born premature. I know these are not all rational thoughts, but I share them with you so you can understand what another person might be feeling. I am not ashamed to say that I have recently reached out in order to receive some counseling. I think it is important for us to know that it is not only normal to have these feelings, but that therapists have helped other people work through them and will be able to do the same for you.

Another important form of self-care for me is having what I call my joy activities. People that know me well know that I am a little over the top when it comes to my calendar planning. I have things synced and color-coordinated between my online calendar and my paper calendar (Yes, I still use a paper calendar. I like being able to see everything in front of me at one time without having to swipe back and forth.). I have different colors for different categories. For instance anything that has to do with my family is orange. Things that are business in nature are yellow, self care items like going to the chiropractor or getting a massage are blue, and my devotional time and religious life is notated in pink. Purple is the color that I love the most!

On my calendar, purple is my joy time. These events might look like girls night at my house, going to coffee with a dear friend, or taking a sushi date with my daughter. When I look at a power-packed week that is full of multiple yellow and oranges with a dash of blue and pink, and I see a large square of purple sitting on Saturday night waiting for me, it helps me to push through all the agenda items that I have that week. I want to make sure that I accomplish everything that I wanted to get done so that when I get to that time of joy, I can truly be present in that moment and just savor whatever it is.

This is advice can apply to everyone. You do not need to have children, you do not need to have a spouse, you just need to be able to give yourself not only a break, but to give yourself some *joy*. I do not believe that anyone can truly find balance in life. There is always going to be an ebb and flow to it. Some weeks will be heavier in certain colors for me. However, finding those moments of joy makes the work we did to get to that point so much more valuable.

Things I Would Do Differently Today: Today, I think I am more sure of myself and aware of my emotions, so I would not be afraid to seek professional help. I also would make sure that I kept daily Me Time and exercise on my schedule every single day. I know that when one or the other of these drop away, it has a great effect on me and my psyche. I would engage more in social time with girlfriends or play in a sports league. That time outside the home is so important as well.

SAY SOMETHING OR SAY NOTHING

I have this girlfriend whom I wish I talked to more, because she always leaves me better than she found me. A true girl scout, right? Her peppy "Hey girl, Hey!" messages crack me up. The thing I appreciate most about her is she is so not an 'askhole.' You know what I mean? Some people just want and want from you. Energy Vampires. Mood Hoovers. They suck it right out of you.

The first time I got a message from her, she claimed all she wanted was to say hi because she was thinking of me. I was perplexed! Who does that anymore? In our digital age and on demand culture, who reaches out just because? But she did and she does. It can shift my entire mood just to hear a friendly voice on the other end of the phone. This is where I am talking to you as friends, family, school support, etc.

There are many of you reading this book who may not be the parent of a child with special needs. That's okay, I'm glad you're here anyway! It could be that you are just reading this because you thought it sounded intriguing. Maybe you're reading this because you do have someone in your life that has a chronic illness or disability, so you are looking for a little insight into their world. If so, this chapter is for you.

It is important for the parents of a child with disabilities to still feel acknowledged. Many times they step back from their known communities. They feel overwhelmed. It can feel like they are out of sight, out of mind. This is typically not the case at all, but that doesn't mean their perception doesn't allow them to think it. That is why connecting with them is important.

There have definitely been times where I just did not know what to say to a friend. Perhaps they were posting about a sick child, or perhaps they lost a loved one. I have always been taught it does not matter if you fumble on the words, just say something. Sometimes honesty really is the best policy. It's better to say "I wish I knew what to say, but I just wanted you to know I was thinking about you," or "I don't know what you're feeling, but I do want you to know that I care," than to say nothing at all.

Simple words, really. I do try to say something. When I see a friend has lost a loved one, I always try to write a note. It may not even be right when it happens, often it is later when the attention is gone away and they are still feeling lost and alone. I try very hard to remember them then.

In a way, being a special needs parent can be kind of like losing a loved one. I don't want to say that I am in any way comparing the loss of a child to getting to raise one. I know that no matter what I say here, some will misconstrue my words and say I made the comparison. That is not my intention at all. However, it is the loss of what you believe the future would be, and that can be hard to deal with. There is a poem that has long been a favorite of mine, and I like to pass it on to new Mamas or someone that is struggling. It is by Emily Perl Kingsley, and in it she describes the anticipation of going to Italy but instead you end up in Holland. It is not at all what you had planned. An excerpt reads:

"It's just a different place. It's slower-paced than Italy, less flashy than Italy. But after you've been there for a while and you catch your breath, you look around.... and you begin to

notice that Holland has windmills....and Holland has tulips. Holland even has Rembrandts.

But everyone you know is busy coming and going from Italy... and they're all bragging about what a wonderful time they had there. And for the rest of your life, you will say 'Yes, that's where I was supposed to go. That's what I had planned.'

And the pain of that will never, ever, ever, ever go away... because the loss of that dream is a very very significant loss."

There are bloggers out there who talk about how awful this poem is. I've heard people ask why on earth any parents would say they are in mourning. Their child is alive, how dare they?! Again, I would never change or trade Colton for the world. Many parents of children with disabilities feel the same.

However, due to his disabilities, things are not ever going to be easier for him. He will work harder just to do things that come quite easily to most. Things people take for granted, buttoning a shirt or tying your shoes. Walking down a hall. Trying to read facial cues and understanding appropriate social exchanges. Every parent wants to see their child succeed in life, yet the dreams we had imagined for his success had to shift into a new picture and be reframed as something else.

It is human nature to want to help our friends and loved ones out. Often times we don't know what to say. It can be a dark and isolating world sometimes as a parent. We all want to be seen and heard. I'm going to try to gather my thoughts of some of the best (and worst) things that have ever been said to me. Here are some of my best ideas in order to help someone that is caring for a sick or disabled family member:

- Do offer to run an errand for them.
- Do offer to make a meal. With all the cool meal train apps available online today, it is such a blessing to be able to take just this one small thing off their plate. It may be easy for you, but I know in the weeks after my son had surgery as a teenager, I was completely overwhelmed with his round-the-clock care. People bringing meals was a lifeline for me.
- Take them a current magazine for reading materials. These are not things they probably have time to stop and look at as they make a mad dash in their errands during the day, however with medical or therapy appointments sometimes it's nice to have something new to look at.
- Offer to sit with them at the hospital or medical appointments, but don't be offended if they say no. Sometimes they may be too exhausted to feel like playing "host," yet if you ask another day they might enjoy the company.
- Check in with them before popping in. Their child may have a therapist or be sleeping. Heck, they as the parent or caregiver may be getting a much needed nap. Again, it goes back to they may not be up for being a host.
- Offer to take their other children home from activities. It saves them from packing up their child, who may have so much equipment and gear that it takes longer to pack and unpack them than it does to actually drive. It takes a village, for sure.
- Send a simple card - for families that get medical bills constantly, it's just such a treat to get real snail mail! Children especially love getting cards so don't feel you need to send it to the parent. Send it direct to the child.

Here are a few Don'ts:

- *Please* don't message us offering us the newest breakthrough fad that is going to "cure" our child. Show love and compassion. I once had someone message me and say, *"I don't know what is wrong with Colton, but I'm sure my XYZ product will fix it."* You have got to be kidding me! XYZ product might actually have been pretty good, but the way it was stated was not the way to soften my heart towards any sort of conversation. Always convey empathy.
- Which leads to the next: Don't say 'that Downs syndrome baby.' That autistic child. That retarded guy. *They are people.* You hopefully don't use rude adjectives when describing people in general conversation. I would hope never to hear someone say "You know that cancer girl checker at the grocery? Do you know that one legged guy at the bank?" Their diagnosis is NOT an adjective. It is a medical condition. I have a son with a diagnosis of cerebral palsy. There is a difference. He wants to be seen as a person first.
- Don't say he or she looks "normal" or "you would never know to look at him/her". What does normal look like anyway? I know plenty of people who are magazine worthy if we are talking strictly physical attributes, but have horrible personalities!
- Don't forget to ask the parent how they are doing too. It is an exhausting job and hearing someone is thinking about you does help.
- Don't assume that certain toys or sporting equipment is not fun for children that have a handicap. I LOVE watching a girl at our sports league who only has use of one arm play basketball, and I have also seen her swim faster than most as well. A young man with Down Syndrome can CRUSH a homerun to the fence in our

softball league. My feelings were hurt many times when people assumed my child could not play sports, so we were not included. Just like those who have had a stroke or perhaps have a prosthetic limb, children with unique abilities find a way to enjoy sports and activities just like everyone else!

- Don't say that your uncle's cousin's brother in law knew someone with "that disability". Each disability is so unique. Even people with the same exact medical diagnosis will have different levels of severity and expression. It would be like saying that everyone with blonde hair is the same, and I think by now most of us are over the lameness of blonde jokes.
- Don't think we always need space. Sometimes being alone only makes the problems worse.

Here is a final Do: convey empathy. It's like the old adage to walk a mile in someone else's shoes. No matter what we have going on in life, there is someone that always has it worse. I will never forget the time that I took Colton to Shriners Hospital to get fitted for his first set of AFOs (little orthotic plastic braces that helped stretched out his heel cords so that he was not walking on his toes). The weeks leading up to the appointment, I was so sad that my son was going to have these little braces, even though I knew it was going to help him walk. When my mom and I got to the hospital, instead of seeing a room full of happy spirited children, we saw multiple toddlers being fitted for prosthetics, as well as many young children who were burn victims. I was absolutely devastated for them and ashamed of myself. How dare I be so selfish to be sad for Colton and his little plastic braces that he would only wear for a short time? These children were dealing with so much more. It was a day that I was glad I did not have to walk a mile in their parent's shoes. Because of days like that one, I am inspired to do more for other parents like those. I want to walk beside them and offer hope and support.

Things I Would Do Differently Today: I am not sure there is a lot I would do differently. Because of exposures to all sorts of different people of all abilities growing up, I do feel I am a compassionate person. I have already mentioned how I tend to take empathy to the next level. I guess if I had to pick anything, it would be to use my influence earlier in my parenting journey. I would help to bring awareness and understanding to people so they might have clarity for what others might be experiencing. Be a voice for those who either can't, won't, or don't speak up for themselves. Be more courageous in knowing that other people's opinions really don't matter. When you know the truth and are convicted in it, it's your obligation to share with others. I hope that you'll do the same. Overflow empathy and compassion until everyone around you does, too.

FINAL JEOPARDY

As a lover of all things game shows, my beloved Colton could give many analogies for the end of this book, but I think he would enjoy it most if I called it Final Jeopardy. You know the game. A clue is given, and you must answer it in question form. Fun categories like the Daily Double challenge you to take risks, to take everything you have learned and put it on the line. Here's the thing, even if you take the risk and you fail in the Daily Double, you are still in the game. The same holds true for life. We can take risks that lead to setbacks or failures, but life continues on. We are not out of the game.

This is the part where I hope I have been vulnerable enough to teach something important. It warms my heart no matter if you had twenty takeaways from this book or just one. But I do hope you had one. Because if each *one* of us can influence *one* other who continues on to influence *one* more, the one simple change we each made creates a ripple effect that causes lasting change. I always pray that my heart for helping others will cause me to be braver than I want to be. I want to be a part of making changes for the good.

I will always be grateful to a certain priest in my life. He had been at my parish when I was a child. I had always been appreciative for his kindness and the way he could relate stories to help me learn and navigate through my teenage years. I saw him again about twelve years ago. I don't even recall the reason for the occasion, but a number of area priests came to our

Church to bestow the Sacrament of Reconciliation. For non-Catholics, you may know the term better as going to confession. For whatever reason, I decided to go that night. We had just been through another medical trial, and my heart was hurting so badly.

I'm pretty sure that all I did when I entered the room was ugly cry for several minutes, and then I began to explain the most recent diagnosis my child had received. The priest lovingly listened, and with great insight told me, "You have a decision to make moving forward from today. I am sure you have spent many of the past few years wondering why this is happening to you. Now it is time to understand why *not* you. You can either continue to ask for Colton's entire life why this happened to you and why this happened to him, and it literally will eat you alive. Or, you can make the choice to decide why not me, and you can go out into the world and let your light shine on others. You can raise your child the best way you know how, and help other people navigate through their hardships. You can actually be a walking, living, breathing example of Christianity for others."

Are you kidding me? Say why not me? Be an example for others? This was deep! I would love to say that right away the ceiling opened up, the skies parted, and a light shone down from heaven above to tell me that, yes indeed, this was the answer I had been looking for. That didn't happen. But I did take into consideration what he was saying. I just was not sure that I wanted that burden yet. That sounded like a lot of work. How could I be an example for others when I was struggling to find someone to be an example for me? Who was going to show *me* the way? I thought about the stories I knew to be true. Of mothers raising their children with unique abilities with strength and grace in a time with less support than what I had. I thought of the commitment my husband and I made to never fall into the 85% and put our marriage first. I thought about all we had overcome so far in such a short time. So I took his advice and I switched my thinking. Why me? Why not me?

It was freeing. Would I tell you I no longer had pain in my heart? Of course not. But when you feel that you have a mission and a purpose, it makes your pain at least feel worth it. You can take that pain and create an opportunity. You can use it to teach others a lesson. You can show the world your triumphs and how you are not just surviving, but thriving. So here it is.

The Final Clue: This author's story impacted the masses, giving people hope for navigating life in a lighthearted way, while fiercely being a champion warrior and advocate for those that needed a voice.

Answer: Who is **You**.

I might be the author of this particular story, but you have a story as well. Each time you are brave enough to tell it, you help someone see light at the end of their tunnel. You help give them freedom and courage. Speak up. You matter. Your story matters. It could be the key to unlock someone else's prison. Your experiences are unique. Someone out there is waiting to listen. Don't get stuck in the Why me? mindset. Claim it today.
Why *not* me?!

ACKNOWLEDGEMENTS

This project would never have happened without some exceptional people in my life. They are the people that share in my sorrow and joys. They love me well and gave me the confidence to know my story matters. This tale has been in my heart, growing and developing for years. They have been there in trenches with me encouraging me to let my own light shine.

So many people inspire me daily! Wonderful organizations that advocate for the inclusion of all people: people from different cultures, religions, and abilities. My world is better because of special people who go out and give a voice to those who cannot. I celebrate you!

Thank you to my "Mama Tribe" who said yes to being all in, giving feedback, talking through ideas, and helping to continually promote this project: Gina Zervos, Kate DeLong, Karren Johnson, Becky Gilbert, Amber Harness, Jamie Mercer, Christine Thompson, Amy Filteau, Alice Hardin, Courtney Veazey-Currie, Leslie Thom, Dawn Scheiderer, and Amy DuMont. I am so grateful to you, Mamas. I know there is more excitement to come. *You are my people*! You live with me in struggles, you are on the other end of the phone for my tears or excitement, and have been an important part of my family's journey.

I continue to be inspired by you, Loren Lahav. There is hardly a twenty-four hours in my life that I can say I learned so much about myself. A vision was born: I am forever grateful!

Thank you to the people that agreed to take the challenge and dive in within such a short amount of time. You've helped push this project out in what had to be record time! I am grateful for Self-Publishing School and my big-hearted coach, Marcy. My words came to life because of the creative genius of my editor, Nicole. Steven pushed this into e-book in record time! Thank you, sir!

Thank you to my sweet friend, Megan Martin, for the most precious forward. The first time I read it I was snorting with laughter, then crying within moments! Playmates are important for everyone at all ages, and I am so lucky to have found you.

I hardly know where to begin when it comes to my soul sister, Brandy Foss. Every time I seem to say, "I just need someone to believe in me" there you are. Countless hours on phone calls, thinking things through together, being a shoulder to cry on or ear to listen. I love that we experience life together, we have playtime and work time, and that my kids call you Auntie Brandy. You have been there for my saddest days, yet been the one I call with my greatest excitements. There wasn't even a moment of hesitation for you to dive head first into this project with me - I pray everyone has a person in their life like I have in you. I love you so very much!

I believe my mom shaped my passion and fierceness about being an advocate for my children. She disciplined us, but she was a very present parent. She always showed up for her kid's events and continues to do so for her grandchildren. I know she sacrificed so that we could experience so much. My dad is the calmest and most patient man I know. His dry humor and powerful commitment to faith influence me still today. They took their marriage vows seriously and have shown what an unbreakable covenant should look like. Taking those traits from them continues to help me be the best parent that I can be to my own kids and wife I can be to Josh.

Owen, my Hurricane, you bring me such happiness each day! Your silliness and wit make you so fun to be around. I know someday you will be a famous youtuber-convenience store owner-gamer if that is what you want to be, because you can do anything you set your mind to doing. I believe in you and all that your future holds!

Thalia, my mini-me, you make me so proud. You are such an encourager to others, and I always pray I haven't pushed too hard because I have always needed you as much as you needed me. The lyrics from Martina McBride's song In my Daughter's Eyes always make me think of you. *"But the truth is plain to see, she was sent to rescue me, I see who I want to be, In my daughter's eyes".* You will accomplish great things, I know!

Colton, the day you were born I knew my life would be forever changed. I did not know what that meant at the time, but the last 18 years you have helped me to practice kindness, compassion, empathy, and to put other people first. You make me laugh so hard, even when I know I should be more firm. Most of all, you have taught me through your Colton's Corner vlog to always "Stay Classy." I know if we can teach more people to do that, the world will be better than we found it. Your future is going to be so full of wonder and excitement! I cannot wait to experience it with you!

Joshua, I don't suppose when you sat down for an Alex's pizza with an old friend that St.Patrick's Day weekend in 1995, you had any idea that you would end up marrying her, much less experience the heartaches and joys that raising a family together has brought. There is no one I can imagine doing life with except you. You keep me on my toes, and never fail to surprise me. I am so grateful for the sacrifices and countless hours you've put in to make sure your wife and children can continue to live out their dreams. Thank you for being my husband, protector, caregiver, soulmate, and the best friend in the world. I'll love you forever!

ABOUT THE AUTHOR

Karen Richards is most proudly a wife to Josh and mother to Colton, Thalia, and Owen. They have served as her inspiration for the stories she writes as well as her journey into health, fitness, and nutrition. As a family, they love traveling, especially to the beach. She and her family reside in Clarksville, TN.

From the age of fifteen, Karen has actively coached and guided participants through many aspects of fitness. She has served as a judge at the national level for cheerleading and dance, as well as coached her own teams. As a personal trainer and fitness instructor, she loved being a part of people getting healthier. She wanted to dive in deeper for people suffering chronic illness and suffering autoimmune diseases like she and her children were.

Karen is the founder and chief executive officer of Karen Richards Health, a practice she enjoys immensely. There she helps people, especially women, create healthier versions of themselves physically, spiritually, and emotionally. Karen believes that the Mama is the heart of the household and wants to keep that heart joyful and vibrant. As a family, the Richards have recently founded Colton's Corner, an organization that is committed to inclusional travel and recreations experiences.

For the past eleven years, Karen has enjoyed leading workshops to help educate others on the power of healthy eating. From parks & recreation conferences, corporate wellness programs, women's wellness retreats, girl scout badge meetings, school and daycare visits, to in-home meal prep workshops,

Karen enjoys seeing people learn a skill or fact they can implement into their daily lives.

Made in the USA
Columbia, SC
22 January 2019